SELF-MARRIAGE

A Ritual for Radical Self-Love

By Megan Taylor Morrison

Let's continue the conversation on Instagram:
@megantaylormorrison
@self_marriage_book

ISBN (softcover): 978-1-7354842-0-4
ISBN (eBook): ISBN: 978-1-7354842-6-6

DEDICATION:

Mom,

You love me as I aspire to love myself. Thank you for demonstrating true care, kindness, and loyalty. Thank you for always believing in me.

CONTENTS

TO READERS:

When I began writing this book, I had no idea self-marriage was a decades-old, worldwide phenomenon. Nor did I realize I would interview dozens of people about their own experiences with this ritual.

I originally put pen to paper for one simple reason: My self-marriage had skyrocketed my sense of self-love...and people had all sorts of questions about the event:

What prompted you to consider "self-marriage"?

What does self-marriage even mean?

How did your family respond when they found out?

What went into planning the ceremony?

How did self-marriage change the way you relate to yourself?

If I want to marry myself, what's the first step?

Through this book, I aimed to provide the answers.

As the first draft came together, however, I felt a strong desire to include other people's stories. I didn't want my experience to seem like the *only* or *right* way to approach self-marriage. I firmly believe each ritual is as unique as the person it honors. Plus, I wanted anyone brave enough to plan their own ceremony to know there are plenty of people who've done it and understand the significance.

So, through the magic of Instagram hashtags (#selfmarriage #imarriedmyself), I found an incredible group of interviewees. Over the next few months, I talked with men and women about the change self-marriage made in their lives. Whether it was a 50-year-old woman in Australia, a 20-something in Uganda or a teenager in California, they'd all had impactful experiences through this ritual. Their stories and photos needed to be a part of this book!

Through my research, I also came across companies that specialize in self-marriages: an enterprise that makes engagement rings for sologomists, people who officiate solo wedding ceremonies and more. What I didn't find, however, was a handbook. There was no guide on how to approach this type of event!

It was then I realized what was truly possible: By sharing about different self-marriages, this book could become a go-to for those inspired by the ritual. In reading about diverse experiences, readers would be better prepared to plan an event that matched their needs and desires. Thus, the fate of the book was sealed. The stories within this manuscript celebrate the many different shapes self-love and self-marriage can take.

Whether you are thinking about having your own ceremony, supporting someone else in their self-marriage, or simply curious about this growing trend, welcome. It's an honor to have you here and a privilege to share the intimate details of so many wedding days.

Embrace the Adventure,

Meg

Watch the interviews

I'll share snippets of each person's self-marriage story in the coming pages. To learn more about these featured guests, head over to my YouTube channel by scanning the QR code to the right. You can watch the entirety of the interviews there. They're full of wisdom bombs, touching stories and fun details, so prepare yourself for a massive dose of inspiration!

INTRODUCTION: WHAT INSPIRED THIS BOOK?

Atlanta (February 23, 2021) I waited patiently in the virtual greenroom of *This Morning*, the largest morning show in the UK, as the production team tested my microphone and sound from afar. I felt both sleepy and excited as I touched up my lipstick and eye shadow. It was 5 a.m. and I would soon be interviewed about my self-marriage in front of a million live viewers.

"You're all set, Meg," a voice whispered through my headset. "You'll be on after the commercials."

~❖~

My appearance on *This Morning* was set in motion by an Instagram post. After my self-marriage, I shared a photo from the event and some initial thoughts about my experience. The post received a typical response of "likes" and comments, but also led to an unexpected email from a man named Martin.

The Instagram Post:

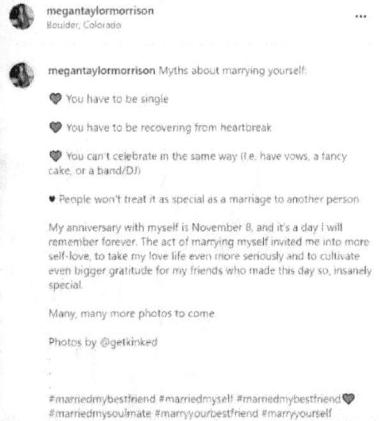

Martin said he was a journalist at Media Drum World (a press agency I had never heard of), and he wanted to share details about my wedding with the publication's readers.

At first, I was dubious. Was this guy for real? While I knew how impactful the event had been on my life, I wasn't sure other people would want to hear about it.

After a few email exchanges, however, Martin seemed pretty legit. And a note from him a week later confirmed my hunch. It read:

> *Hi Meg,*
>
> *I received an email from a UK TV show called* This Morning *(it's the biggest morning TV show in the UK by a long way) inquiring about stories we had available that could suit. I pitched your story, and they are interested in interviewing you on the show to tell the story of your self-marriage. Could this be of interest to you? If so, I shall put you in touch with them to discuss further.*
>
> *Thanks!*

I sat for a moment, staring at Martin's message. Apparently, I'd sorely underestimated how much interest my self-wedding would inspire. Nonetheless, I appreciated the opportunity to talk about how the event had inspired me to overcome people-pleasing, think carefully about how to improve my self-care, set better boundaries, and otherwise improve my life. In fact, in my work as a Professional Certified Coach, this ritual was by far the most potent method I'd found to up-level my self-love. Given that I'd geeked out on countless personal development books and trainings for almost a decade, this was saying something.

Over the next few days, however, I realized *This Morning*'s producers were more interested in using the story as a light-hearted interlude between other segments. They didn't seem to grok how this ritual could be a potent force for good in people's lives.

"We need this to be less serious," one producer said to me after an initial chat about the importance of learning to trust yourself. "Can you give us more of the fun details?"

While I was happy to oblige, I was not willing to forgo the deeper conversation. When I appeared on the show, I promised myself, I would balance lighthearted banter with poignant reflections about the importance of self-love.

~❖~

I was deep in thought, reflecting on the journey thus far, when I heard the program's jingle. It was "showtime."

I took a deep breath as the celebrated hosts, Philip Schofield and Holly Willoughby, began to introduce me.

"Our next guest was left heartbroken when her three-year relationship ended, despite always dreaming of a wedding day," Holly announced.

"However, Meg Taylor Morrison found an unusual way of moving on when she decided to have her own big day and marry herself," Philip said.

For the next six minutes, I answered Philip and Holly's questions about the event, what the wedding meant to me, and whether I planned on marrying someone else in the future.

Holly: "This started with heartbreak, did it?"

Me: "It absolutely did. My partner and I of three-and-a-half years decided to end our relationship this past summer. It was a mutual decision, but mutual decisions don't always make breaking up any easier."

Philip: "And had you talked about marriage?"

Me: "We had, but like a lot of couples during the coronavirus pandemic, we had a lot of conversations about what was next for us. In the end, we decided it wasn't the right fit."

Holly: "So you were recovering from a broken heart, and you started thinking about getting married to yourself?"

Meg: "I'd heard of self-marriages before, and I thought 'why not marry myself?' It could be fun! I decided to turn it into a commitment to self-love, taking care of myself and putting myself first. I think any good relationship – whether it's with ourselves or other people – begins with having more appreciation for ourselves."

Philip: "So you decided to tell your family and your friends. Your mom was a bit unsure about this at first?"

Meg: "She was. She was a little nervous it might be seen as egotistical or that people would take it the wrong way, but we had a great conversation about it. In the end I said, 'This is my chance to put down people-pleasing, to trust myself and what I want, and what I see this difference could make for me and even for others.' Once she got the meaning behind it, she came around. She's my biggest supporter, so I'm not surprised."

Holly: "You had to be open to friends helping you and let go of control. You said that was an important lesson in self-love."

Meg: "That was the biggest gift I gave myself during the wedding – releasing any attachment to how things would go, which was great because we had a wedding cake disaster and lots of things didn't go as planned. In the end, because I'd already decided it would all be perfect, I got to relax and have a wonderful day."

Philip: "Then there is this moment where you walk down the aisle, and I assume you put the ring on your own finger? We see you kissing the mirror there when you can 'kiss the bride.'"

Me: "Yup! I put the ring on my own finger. It was a great time to share that my mom had picked it out and that sometimes self-love means letting other people take care of you. It can be a true community experience. So, I put it on my finger. I said my vows to myself and then I gave myself a big smooch in the mirror."

Holly: "Would you be open to marrying someone else?"

Philip: "But that would mean three people in the marriage! Would you divorce yourself?"

Me: "I don't think I would want to. I'm really enjoying this marriage so far. *And* I would be open to marrying someone else. Any good relationship starts with a good relationship with yourself, so I feel like I'm better prepared for my next partnership."

Philip: "So as you sit here now – a married woman to yourself – what has it changed in your attitude [toward yourself]?"

Me: "I didn't expect the vow I made to myself to release perfectionism and accept things as they are to have such an impact on me. I now understand the purpose of the wedding band – it's a symbol of a commitment you've made. By looking at my ring every day, it helps me set aside perfectionism, to breathe and to enjoy things as they come. It's made life more easeful and lovely."

Holly: "Are you wearing it on the wedding finger?"

Me: "No, I wear it on my middle right finger."

Holly: "So there's room for another one?"

Me (smiling): "Yeah, I still have space for whoever else comes along!"

With that, Philip and Holly said goodbye and I was suddenly alone in the virtual greenroom once again. I felt satisfied. I had stayed true to my plan to have fun and provide poignant reflections.

I had a feeling my segment would be polarizing (given that the producers had told me they had a psychologist available if I needed to talk to her after my segment aired, I imagined they anticipated this too). The ensuing messages I received on Instagram and Facebook did indeed represent both ends of the spectrum. While some people shared how inspired they were, and men from across the world sent me heart and rose emojis, other viewers wrote some downright impressive hate mail that must have required hours of internet trolling.

The Twitter response was also divided. I was either #lifegoals or a complete lunatic. Here are a couple of examples:

Positive response: "This woman on #thismorning has married HERSELF. I want to do this OMG."

Negative: "#ThisMorning cannot believe I'm watching some attention-seeking freak nut job talking about her wedding day when she married herself??"

And so on.

As I watched the reactions flow in, I couldn't help but wonder if the divisiveness over my harmless, sweet ceremony indicated something deeper about society's views on self-love. Why wouldn't putting a ring on your own finger and promising to exquisitely care for yourself be universally celebrated?

Perhaps people saw my decision as an affront to traditional marriage. Did they feel I was making light of that sacred commitment? Or that I didn't understand or respect how it was meant to support a couple?

This was not the case. I fully believe that traditional marriage ceremonies are beautiful and powerful rituals. Many couples I know talk about how momentous it was to read their vows out loud to their partner and witnesses. Numerous people had told me: "It was the best day of our lives!" I believed them and hearing their stories felt inspiring.

Yet, I also heard an opportunity. So much time, energy, and money is dedicated to celebrating bonds between two people. Rarely, however, do people treat a bond with themselves with the same reverence. What I've come to learn is that romantic relationships would be even stronger if we did! People who know how to take fantastic care of themselves are often more capable of setting healthy boundaries and asking for what they need – actions that can make a lifetime union more authentic, satisfying, and sustainable.

Maybe, on the other hand, people were upset about my self-marriage because they thought it was an entirely self-centered act – naval gazing in the extreme. This, however, contradicted one of the core philosophies behind my event: by learning to better love ourselves, we not only enjoy life more, but serve others with greater potency. When you are well-resourced, you can bring greater presence, patience, and compassion to those who need support. For this reason, self-marriage is not a selfish act. When done for the right reasons, it can have a far-reaching positive impact on the lives of those around you.

I didn't invent the idea that nurturing self-love benefits the greater good. This approach has been extolled by the likes of legendary Greek and Chinese philosophers, as well as thought leaders from around the world.

In the 3rd century BC, for instance, Aristotle wrote that one loves another as one loves oneself. Put a different way, by cultivating more self-love, your capacity for love in general expands. Want an example? Imagine that you are well slept, eating nutritious meals and nurturing your greatest passion. From this grounded place, would you be able to bring more patience and understanding to a conflict with someone in your inner circle? Probably.

About hundred years after Aristotle graced the halls of the Lyceum, Jesus shared a similar message with his followers: "Love your neighbor as yourself." If people criticized their neighbors the way they criticize themselves in their own minds, that would make for a miserable block party.

I'll name just one more example (although there are many): the teachings of Confucius. Confucian culture recognized self-love as the starting point and premise to love others.

"Be able to be yourself first, and then help those in need," Confucius said. He laid this out as an aspect of *ren* – the foundational virtue of Confusionism that emphasizes the ideals of goodness, benevolence, and love.

Confucius' teachings were not only influential in the past, but continue to shape how many Chinese perceive and approach self-love. Two studies conducted in 2021 revealed how his teachings influence modern views there:

"[The studies] revealed three important aspects of the Chinese understanding of self-love," the authors wrote. "(1) self-love has four dimensions: self, family, others, and society; (2) it comprises five components: self-cherishing, self-acceptance, self-restraint, self-responsibility, and self-persistence; and (3) the five components of self-love are linked together to form a stable personality structure. Finally, the results showed that Chinese self-love is dominated by Confucian culture, which provides guiding principles for how to be human."

So why else might people be bothered by my self-marriage? It was possible that some wrote it off as the ultimate act of privilege: *What sort of spoiled brat has the money and time for that?*

I get it, especially since in some ways I fit that stereotype. I am white woman who grew up in a middle-class family. And while I did work very hard to earn the money I spent on my ceremony, growing up the way I did helped make my success possible.

Nevertheless, seeing self-marriage as an option only for people of a certain income level misses an important point. You don't need to spend *any* money on the event, nor does it require extensive planning (you'll hear more about how some people kept things free and/or simple in the coming pages).

In the end, no matter why someone objected, I hoped they wouldn't write off self-marriage prematurely. I knew deep in my bones that this ritual could benefit many people if they only knew about it.

Society bombards us with messages that undermine self-love. This includes perpetuating the "perfect body" in magazines, expecting us to work when we (or our children) are sick and need rest, or glorifying all-nighters that undermine basic self-care. In infinite ways, we've been trained to shove self-love aside to serve others' ideals or to feed their bottom line.

This has a real, negative impact on our psyche. Look no further than the abundant statistics about rising stress levels, low self-esteem, increased anxiety, cyber-bullying, and eating disorders to see the way that additional structures to promote self-love could serve our world.

If every person felt empowered to make self-loving decisions (such as setting hours that promote work-life balance or saying "no" to spending time with toxic people), focus on the beauty of who they are (already! right now!), and stand up for their goals, values, and desires, can you imagine how society would change? If self-love became a top priority, our world would become a very different place.

Some of the challenges we face

In many ways, society tells us we are not good enough. Unrealistic expectations perpetuated by sources such as the media and companies more interested in their bottom line than the health of their employees have created institutionalized trauma among people across the planet. Here are some troubling statistics that show the negative impact of these influencers:

1.   According to DoSomething, the largest not-for-profit exclusively for young people and social change, roughly 91 percent of women are unhappy with their bodies and diet to try to achieve their ideal weight. Furthermore, 7 in 10 girls believe that they are not good enough or don't measure up in some way.

2.   In 2016, the personal care brand Dove surveyed 10,500 women and girls across 13 countries to better understand the challenges they face (and therefore, we can safely assume, better market to them). The company concluded that low body esteem is a "unifying challenge

shared by women and girls around the world – regardless of age or geography." Furthermore, nearly 8 in 10 (78%) of both women and girls reported feeling some pressure to never make mistakes or show weakness. Even more worrying, the study showed how these concerns impact a woman's ability to realize her potential. Nearly all women (85%) and girls (79%) said they opt out of important life activities, such as trying out for a team and engaging with loved ones, when they don't feel good about the way they look. Seven out of 10 girls surveyed also said that, if they're not happy with how they look, they won't assert their opinion or stick to their decisions.

3. The Anxiety and Depression Association of America estimates that 264 million people worldwide have an anxiety disorder (and women are nearly twice as likely as men to be diagnosed with an anxiety disorder in their lifetime).

4.   In 2020, compounding stressors – including those caused by the global pandemic – were impacting people at a record rate, according to the American Psychological Association (APA). In fact, the APA reported: "We are facing a national mental health crisis that could yield serious health and social consequences for years to come."

5.   The Royal Society for Public Health recently conducted a survey of nearly 1,500 young people between the ages of 16 to 24 and asked them questions specific to their social media use and their mental health. Seven out of 10 said they had experienced cyber-bullying through social media.

6.   According to the Eating Disorders Coalition, as of 2020, anorexia is the third most common chronic illness among adolescents, after asthma and obesity. The rate of children under 12 being admitted to a hospital for eating disorders rose 119% in less than a decade.

I'm not saying self-marriage is the way to end society's problems or master self-love. There is no silver bullet for either of these challenges and they will require ongoing, dedicated effort. Given this very real state of the world, however, why not promote a ritual that has supported thousands of people across the globe in building self-esteem, cultivating confidence, healing after trauma, and other positive changes? If introducing self-marriage to a wider audience could shift the above statistics even slightly, it's a worthwhile endeavor.

~❖~

Over the next several months, as these thoughts swirled through my mind, I knew that my six minutes on British national television had not been nearly enough time to explain self-marriage. Feeling drawn to share more, I sat down one weekend and outlined this book. I wanted to impart the lessons I'd learned, as well as break down the self-marriage ritual into 10 easy-to-follow steps for anyone interested in pursuing it.

Because this book is not only about self-marriage, but also self-love, it goes beyond my wedding day details. It includes personal stories about my own self-love journey, which date back 15 years and span three continents. This is my way to normalize the ups, downs, and ongoing nature of this adventure – a saga that can include self-marriage as one of its chapters.

Self-love takes practice. It's not a straight or smooth road. Luckily, the path can be made easier with a seasoned mentor. I am delighted to be one of your guides and to share the wisdom I've compiled from my interviews. I believe the anecdotes, tips, paradigms, philosophies, exercises, and practices in the coming pages will be invaluable resources for you.

By the end of this book, you'll have had a few "ah-ha" moments about your relationship to self-love. Plus, you'll be well equipped to plan (or delegate the planning of) your own self-marriage. Furthermore, because the lessons herein can also be applied to your life in general, your dedication to apply what you're learning can result in a personal transformation that lasts far beyond your ceremony.

Let's start a self-love revolution, shall we? It's time to say "I do" to yourself... which ultimately means saying "I do" to better relationships with co-workers, friends, family, and lovers.

Self-love practices:

Journal about the questions below. Or, if you prefer, discuss them with a trusted friend.

1. What does self-love mean to you?

2. In what ways would you like to love yourself better?
3. What frightens you most about the idea of self-marriage?
4. What intrigues you most about the idea of self-marriage?

You're allowed to skip a step!

Before we go any further, I want to give you full, explicit permission to skip any practice in this book that does not feel right to you. Remember: The steps here are meant to be a guide, not the absolute truth of what you need to do to marry yourself. While stepping outside of your comfort zone to do some of the practices might lead to eye-opening experiences or personal growth, you are encouraged to honor your boundaries, too! If something feels like a "no," trust your gut. You can always come back to the practice if you feel inspired by it later.

Why Marry Yourself?

As I've talked to others about their self-marriages, I've enjoyed hearing the many different, empowering reasons they chose this route. Here are just a few examples:

- "As a Black femme it was important for me to choose myself first and put myself first," said Kyisha Williams (34, Toronto, Ontario, anniversary: 1/3/2015). "I received a lot of social messages that I'm not supposed to love myself as much as others. I knew that, in order to keep myself alive, I'd need to prioritize myself and my well-being. I thought self-marriage was a great way to make that real."

- Sarah Proffitt (33, Saint Augustine, FL, anniversary: 2/24/2021) felt like she was constantly giving up on herself. Every time she decided on a goal – whether with her fitness or her business – she'd get halfway to achieving it and then give up. Wanting a ritual that would help her fully commit to her aims, she decided self-marriage was the path she would take.

- From age 35-40, Sasha Cagen (Pawtucket, RI, anniversary: 6/2014) underwent a lengthy healing process through coaching and therapy. She dealt with deep-seated shame (a result of childhood trauma), worked through unhealthy behavioral patterns such as not speaking up for herself and feeling unworthy. Self-marriage provided a ritual to commemorate this phase of inner work and to honor all of herself – including the parts that felt difficult or fragile.

- Britt Lynn LaBouef (32, Las Vegas, NV, anniversary: 2/14/18) self-married two weeks before marrying her husband. She saw her solo ceremony as an opportunity to commit to staying true to herself. This, she believed, was key to a healthy, long-term relationship with someone else. "In the past, I would abandon myself in relationships," Britt Lynn said. A couple of weeks after her solo ceremony, when she was at the altar with her partner, one of Britt Lynn's vows revealed a big shift: "I vow to love, respect and honor myself first and not to look to you as my sole source of happiness." Several years later, Britt Lynn and her husband both believe this promise has strengthened their relationship.

- Jevranne Martel (33, Ottowa, Montreal, anniversary: 9/14/19) endured "years of self-hate" as she tried to conform to other's beauty standards, such as wearing makeup and dying her hair. In 2019, while at a friend's wedding, she realized self-marriage would be a way to reinforce her budding belief that her own desires about her body (and life in general) were worthy and valid. She married herself by the ocean a few months later.

- When his parents divorced, Logan Griffin (35, Santa Barbara, California, 5/25/2005) was just 5 years old. After this difficult time, as well as other challenging events in his early life and teenage years, Logan began therapy. Logan's therapist helped guide him and taught him meditation. Spiritual practices, self-improvement and holistic health became Logan's passions. At age 19, he had a revelation: Everything he was conditioned to seek outside of himself, he could find within, and much of the suffering he experienced was from the story that he needed something outside of himself to be okay. Logan spontaneously came to the idea of self-marriage. He saw it as a way to express his commitment to loving himself first and foremost and standing in his self-sovereignty. Logan believed this would also support his commitment to loving others better, inner equanimity and personal empowerment.

- After her fiancée broke up with her a few months before their wedding in Santorini, Greece, Laëtitia Nguyen (37, Grenoble, France, anniversary: 5/27/17) decided to plan a very different event with their non-refundable deposits. "I needed to be surrounded by friends and family for their support at that difficult time," Nguyen said. Ultimately, her self-marriage was the empowering experience she needed for her next phase of healing and to feel a greater sense of closure.

- Lulu Jemimah (35, Kampala, Uganda, anniversary: 8/27/18) comes from Uganda where people (including strangers) feel free to ask you about when you are getting married. Rather than spend her time dating, however, Lulu wanted to prioritize finishing her master's at Oxford University in the UK. She married herself to remind people that she could get married whenever she wanted and that she had better things to worry about. "It was an attitude of, 'you want a wedding? Well, here you go!'" Lulu said. Later, after careful consideration, Lulu decided to launch a crowdfunding campaign based on the event. She needed to raise enough money to finish her degree and wanted to make a statement: while some people want to get married, others want to pursue education or other dreams.

- Zoe Brooker (44, Healdsburg, CA, anniversary: 6/7/2014) had just separated from her husband when she decided to marry herself. "I struggled through the relationship the whole time," she explained. "I'd put [my husband] on a pedestal, give up on my own aspirations, and wasn't in touch with my needs. It was very codependent." While the break-up was devastating, Zoe recognized an opportunity. Self-marriage could be part of her journey in getting to know herself again.

- While waiting in line at the courthouse for her brother's wedding, Kim Parrales (34, North Bergen, NJ, anniversary: 12/30/19) wondered, "What would it be like to marry myself?" As she thought it through, she realized it was a chance to reinforce who she wanted to be in the world: to pursue goals from a place of love and inspiration, to be true to herself, to always give 100 percent not only to others but also to herself, and to always strive to be a better person. She married herself on the spot without an audience or spending a cent. The event was commemorated by a photo snapped by a friend.

- For Amy Kayla (27, Austin, TX, anniversary: 5/21), self-marriage was a chance to establish a sense of equanimity within herself. "My life revolved around the idea of marriage and attracting the interest of the 'right' person," Amy said. "When I found myself without any partner for the first time in a long time, I [experienced] a deep lacking. I posed the question to myself 'What would happen if I treated myself as a whole person or a whole marriage?'" Amy called her self-marriage "a grounding experience" that has allowed her to discover and embrace who she is outside of a romantic partnership.

Watch the interviews:

Do you want to meet the love of your life? Look in the mirror.
— Byron Katie

The author read her vows while looking at herself in a beautiful, mango wood mirror held up by a friend. Behold the kiss at the end!
Photo credit: Geof Krum.

STEP 1:

BEGIN YOUR COURTSHIP

S ydney, Australia (August 2006) – As I walked into the movie theatre, the awkwardness set in. Taking a seat in an empty row, I wondered if anyone noticed I'd arrived alone. Best case scenario: they would think my boyfriend was out buying me a soda at the concession stand. Worst case: someone was feeling sorry for me for coming by myself.

Maybe she doesn't have any friends. I imagined them thinking. Or: *No boyfriend? Did she just get dumped?*

I looked at my watch, unsure how to act nonchalant when I felt so self-conscious.

Can this movie start, already? I wondered impatiently. I couldn't wait for the lights to dim so I would disappear.

The real reason I'd gone stag that evening was simple. It was 2006, and I had just arrived in Sydney, Australia, for the independent study portion of my study abroad program. Because I was brand new to the city, I didn't yet know anyone. Nevertheless, I was dying to go see the Russell Crowe film *A Good Year*.

I'll just go by myself, I thought. *That should be fun, right?*

Wrong. As I sat through the previews, I felt more and more uncomfortable. I'd never taken myself out before, and this attempt was as cringeworthy as my first date in high school. I wasn't sure how to act, what the "rules" were, or what I wanted when there was no one else around. That night, at age 20, I was beginning to notice that I lacked the confidence to spend time with the person who mattered most: myself.

As the drumroll to the 20th Century Fox introduction played, I felt like I was ceremoniously inducted into the next chapter of personal growth: one in which I had the opportunity to purposefully cultivate more personal empowerment by courting myself.

~❖~

It's a terrible disservice to all people that society doesn't teach and encourage us to date ourselves – not as a substitute for dating others, but as a way to better understand who we are and how to embrace our desires, needs, and values.

In cultivating this self-knowledge, we become better at identifying what we want, asking for it, and setting healthy boundaries. We're also much less likely to fall into patterns of people-pleasing, approval-seeking, self-doubt and settling for less than we deserve. All of this makes for a more fulfilling life. Plus, when well resourced, we are often better prepared to give back to our loved ones and society in a thoughtful way.

To drive home the positive potential of self-dating, consider the following scenario.

Imagine a high school course on this subject. Each week, the instructor gives students a list of activities (attend a cooking class, visit a museum, go to a coffee shop and read a book, try yoga, make yourself a picnic, keep a gratitude journal, order a dish you've never tried at a local restaurant, volunteer for a cause you care about, etc...) with the following assignment:

Review these activities and secretly do one each week that you believe will bring you joy. Do it alone and do not discuss your experience with others so that you will not be influenced by others' opinions. If you talk about what you chose to do or how it went with anyone before the end of the semester, it is an automatic "fail." To "ace" this assignment, keep a journal in which you write briefly about your experience before, during, and after the activity. In your writing, make sure to answer the following three questions:

- *How did it feel to make a choice based only on what you felt inspired to do?*

- *What did you learn about yourself throughout the experience?*

- *How was this different from going out with friends?*

What do you think students would learn after just one semester?

What do you think *you* would learn if you took this class? Would you discover a difference between what you enjoy and what you *think* you *should* enjoy? Perhaps you'd realize that you have very different preferences when you're the only person to please. It could also be that you have a few lightbulb moments about new things you love or additional self-care practices that make you feel amazing.

Start to consider what life would be like if you were navigating the world via your inspiration, rather than an obligation to other people's preferences. Of course, I don't mean you should be selfish and always want your own way – compromise is an essential part of life – but it's important to understand your own true desires so that you know how to nurture yourself when the time is right. You'd be surprised by how many people aren't aware of what they want.

If self-dating was a required class, I believe people would better understand how to make more satisfying choices about their hobbies and career trajectories, not to mention finding friends and partners better suited to who they really are. So, since we weren't lucky enough to have this as part of our schooling, why not simulate it now?

Self-courtship is the adult version of the high-school course I just described, and you can kick it off anytime using the "homework" prompt I outlined above. Each date is a data point and will teach you more about yourself as long as you take the time to reflect on it. It will help you build muscles around identifying and owning what you want, which will be key to planning your self-marriage.

Simple Self-Dates

While I listed several examples of self-dating in the exercise described above, here are a few additional no-to-low-cost activities that fit the bill (self-love doesn't have a price tag).

1. Get into bed earlier than you otherwise would. Read a book or magazine, watch a show you love or simply allow yourself to drift off so you get extra sleep.
2. For a full day, give yourself permission to say "no" to any requests you receive that don't *truly* feel like a yes.
3. Volunteer a few hours of your time to a cause you care about.

4. Take walks at the end of the day without your phone. Give yourself space to think. If you'd prefer a walking meditation, keep your focus on how it feels to move and the sensation of your feet hitting the ground. The app Calm has a great guided walking meditation, too.

5. Embrace your creative side by drawing, painting, sculpting, or making bouquets of flowers (enjoy them yourself or give them to someone you love as a surprise).

6. Stay in bed later than you usually do in the morning. Give yourself permission to do whatever you want: play on your phone, browse though a magazine, etc...

7. Take a long bath in the evening. You can add essential oils, bubbles or whatever else feels nourishing.

If you opt for a wedding that involves lots of people and details (like I did), you will need to make dozens of important decisions about that day, such as the location, theme, dress code, whom to invite, the song for your first dance and much more.

Or you might realize through your self-dating that you prefer to have a no-frills ceremony with just one guest. That single important decision will ensure you don't spend money and time on something that doesn't truly matter to you.

No matter which way you go, if you've taken the time to get to know yourself, making choices will be quicker and easier. Plus, since the average American adult makes about 35,000 decisions each day, your courtship will improve your decisiveness in general. What a nice side effect, right?

Diving Deep

While for many people it's an act of self-love to keep self-courtship simple, others feel inspired to dive deep into this process. The two women below decided to take the latter route. As you read their approach, remember that self-love is a process. You don't need to put pressure on yourself to be in the perfect place before your self-marriage. Instead, you can begin and continue the process via date nights after you say "I do!"

- Laetitia Casano (40, Barcelona, Spain, anniversary: 10/28/2018) said her self-courtship was more like self-development. To get to know herself better, she went to psychotherapy and alternative therapies (such as family constellations, kinesiotherapy and hypnosis) and women's circles focused on topics, such as feminine empowerment. Through this exploration, she came to better understand who she was at her best, as well as discovered the ways she sabotaged her own happiness.

"I realized I had an addiction to drama in my relationships, which looked many different ways, including regularly breaking up with someone and then getting back together with them," Laetitia said. "All the drama and intensity, this is what I had seen from my parents' relationship growing up."

In addition, she discovered a discrepancy in how she approached the world when single as opposed to while in a romantic partnership. "I am typically a strong, independent, opinionated woman," she said. "When I would get into relationships, however, I would become a little girl, looking for a prince charming to make my life better." For Laetitia, recognizing these patterns was the first step in shifting them.

- Robbie Fincham (55, Melbourne, Australia, anniversary: 2/7/2021) believed it was critical to cultivate a closer relationship with herself before her self-marriage. Why? She wanted to be ready to look at herself in the mirror and sincerely say, "I love you." Because she so often suffered from an inner voice that said she was not good enough, Robbie decided it would be helpful to learn to use meditation to quiet her critical mind. Through various courses and reading/researching, she cultivated the ability to meditate, at one stage for several hours a day. In addition, she spent ample quality time with herself through activities she loved, and which brought her closer to nature, including gardening and hiking. Thanks to this work, on her wedding day, Robbie felt ready to commit to a "life-long love affair" with herself.

~❖~

My movie theatre experience catalyzed my own crash course in self-dating. It was so pivotal that, as Russel Crowe's character went through his own life-changing experience renovating a vineyard in Provence, I was only half watching.

There in the dark, my own "a-ha" moment got my attention. I realized how uncomfortable I was spending time alone, since I believed others would label it as "wrong," "weird," or "pathetic." Most interestingly: If I took my imaginary audience out of the equation, I realized I was quite happy to be by myself.

Most likely, no one that day was paying me the slightest attention. But insecurities that we harbor, as I did then, can make us feel as if a bright spotlight has been aimed at us and everyone knows exactly what we are thinking and feeling.

It's crazy that this bias against spending time alone has been floating around in my mind, I thought. *What else have I been missing out on? What activities would I have pursued if I'd felt more confident doing them without having someone else along?*

While I couldn't control the past, I knew it wasn't too late to rewrite this story. Learning to love spending time with myself would be key to my future goals of traveling solo around the world and cultivating a romantic relationship in which my partner and I valued our relationship with ourselves as much as our relationships with one another.

When the lights went on in the movie theatre two hours later, I asked myself a simple question: *What would make you happy now?*

The answer was to take a long walk, so I did. Then, I wanted to go out for Indian food. So, I did. While I never felt totally at ease, my awareness of the disempowering belief at the root of my discomfort took the edge off. By understanding myself better, I could adjust my self-talk in a supportive way: *It's OK that this feels weird. Take some deep breaths. You're just learning to spend time with yourself, and this is unfamiliar territory. Can you appreciate where you are right now? You've taken the first step! Embrace the awkward!*

By the time the night was over, I had already planned my next self-date: coffee and reading at a cute cafe near Bondi Beach. Thus, a few days later, I settled in at a shady table in the landmark Sydney neighborhood.

Ordering a decaf latte, I kicked off a sweet morning of reading and people-watching. An hour later, as I checked in with myself, I realized I felt significantly less awkward than I had on my first self-date! While I occasionally still wondered what others might be thinking about me, it didn't pull my attention away from enjoying the breeze on my skin and *Harry Potter*.

Over the next six months, I balanced socializing with friends and self-dating until one day I realized I looked forward to my time alone just as much as my time with others!

While learning to embrace my courtship required an intentional process, it was well worth it. My initial experience in Australia helped me build the confidence to embark on many other incredible solo adventures. I traveled through East Africa (including summiting Kilimanjaro and doing a stint in Madagascar working for the World Wildlife Fund); I moved to the Dominican Republic to study bachata (a local dance now enjoyed worldwide) and applied to a journalism graduate school program at Northwestern University that made me ecstatic. These experiences shaped me personally and professionally, and I would have missed out on them if I hadn't had the self-knowledge I'd gained from spending time alone.

Too often, we wait for someone to go with us or to tell us that something's a good idea. The experience of self-courtship can help you throw this behavioral pattern out the window. Give yourself the gift of more self-knowledge. It will not only make it easier to cultivate your own joy but will make sure you're ready to bring the authentic you to future dates with another person, if that's what you desire. At the very least, the experiences of your solo dates will lead to memories you treasure. Plus, they can provide great material for your vows!

Self-love practices:

- Plan self-dates: Start with a single outing and then continue this ritual at least once or twice a month for as long as you can (hopefully forever!). Over time, you'll build confidence identifying what you want and doing wonderful things for yourself. Use the practice I outlined* earlier in this chapter:

1) choose an activity you think sounds fun;

2) do it;

3) reflect on the experience afterward using these three questions:

- What was it like to make a choice based only on what you felt inspired to do?

- What did you learn about yourself throughout the experience?

- How was this different from going out with friends?

Feel free to modify these questions or add to them!

*This practice was inspired by Julia Cameron's bestselling book, *The Artist's Way,* in which she encourages a form of self-courtship that she calls Artist's Dates. Artist's dates feed the senses and encourage inspiration, something we can all use in our daily lives.

Decide whether or when you want to pop the question!

Once you've become comfortable dating yourself, consider if you'd like to propose. While I simply decided to marry myself and then moved forward with planning, many others have found fun ways to ask for their own hand in marriage.

- A *Canadian Broadcasting Corporation* article described how Ottawa resident Jen Harju proposed to herself during a hot air balloon ride in Las Vegas (much to the surprise of the unsuspecting German tourists sharing that experience with her). The proposal was filmed by documentary filmmaker Amen Jafri who was chronicling Harju's self-marriage journey.

- Alex Christopher Strand (52, Varberg, Sweden, anniversary: 5/28/2020) proposed to himself at home in Sweden on a cold, winter night. He made it special by dressing up and preparing a lovely dinner. He served himself a vegetarian pasta dish and nonalcoholic rosé, followed by a post-meal espresso with chocolate pralines.

- Chinese woman Feng Jinjin threw herself a red-themed engagement party. At the event, she announced to a group of her girlfriends that she would marry herself, and that this was a part of finding and liking herself. Jinjin's story was reported in a 2019 edition of the *South China Morning Post.*

- Sasha Cagen enjoyed an impromptu engagement at the end of her birthday road trip to hot springs in the California desert. She had been thinking about proposing to herself all weekend but had felt too shy to do it. When Sasha and her friends made a pit stop, she knew this was her chance. The shop at the gas station was full of self-help books, jewelry, and other gifts. When she saw a necklace that said "Love, Alexandra" (her birth name) she purchased it. The engagement was followed by a photo shoot in the parking lot.

Check out my interviews with people about
their self-marriage experience:

Love yourself first and everything else falls into line. You really have to love yourself to get anything done in this world.
— *Lucille Ball*

Jevranne Martel in her self-marriage dress at Red Rock Beach on Prince Edward Island in Canada.
Photo credit: Yolande Williams

STEP 2:

CLARIFY YOUR COMMITMENTS

S himoni, Kenya (April 2009) – "You're on squat toilets this week, Meg."

I grimaced as the manager at our remote field camp in Kenya assigned me the most dreaded chore. For the next seven days, I would have to keep the shared bathrooms squeaky clean. Given that many people were having GI issues as they adjusted to the new environment, this felt like a true sacrifice for my fellow volunteers.

While I'd like to say that I jumped at the chance to show off my poop-plowing prowess, this simply wasn't the case. Full disclosure: when I heard my task for the week, part of me wanted to hop back on the rickety bus that had dropped us all off a few days earlier.

Peace out, everybody! I could hear myself saying, as the *matutu* rumbled slowly toward Nairobi. *I'm headed back to the magical land of flush toilets!*

A bigger part of me, however, was up for the task. Why? My decision to come here, freshly graduated from college, was based on my deep commitment to serving a cause I believed in. While in East Africa, I would survey animals for the Kenya Wildlife Service, a critical task that supported local conservation efforts. My less-than-glamorous assignment, it turned out, was an unadvertised part of the job.

Remembering the larger goal, and that every choice we make has upsides and drawbacks, I pulled a handkerchief over my nose, grabbed a mop, and began the long walk down the hallway toward the bathrooms.

When I emerged an hour later, the sincere thanks I received from my peers made me feel the work had been worth it. We were a team, and – while I would never come to enjoy this intimate relationship with our squat toilets – I began to see that I could find satisfaction in caring for my fellow volunteers and sacrificing for something I believed in.

By the end of my stay at the field camp in Kenya, I'd developed a belief that still guides my decisions today: When we follow our commitments, we often are led outside our comfort zone and achieve a more fulfilling version of life.

~❖~

Our commitments serve as a North Star, and this is true whether we are deep in the African savannah or preparing for self-marriage. After all, at its core, a wedding is a commitment ritual. When two people get married, they commit to leading a life together, even when the going gets tough. Those commitments become the foundation upon which everything else can rest.

The same principle applies when you marry yourself. Rather than jumping straight into the juicy details about where the event will be and who you'll invite, start by constructing the skeleton. What are the important commitments that your special day memorializes?

To make your list, you might first consider the ways in which you undermine your own self-love or self-confidence. Once you've found what *doesn't* work, you can create commitments that set you up for a more positive life experience (I'll walk you through this process in the practices section at the end of this chapter).

Here are some other examples of how you can turn challenges into commitment opportunities:

Challenge	Commitment
I'm very hard on myself	I will treat myself with the same forgiveness and compassion I give to others
I take my accomplishments for granted	I will pause to acknowledge and celebrate my accomplishments, taking time to savor the progress I've made
I'm exhausted from taking care of everyone else	Though I will continue to be considerate of others, I will put on my own proverbial oxygen mask first

I'm a workaholic	I will set boundaries with my work that allow me to take part in activities that I find deeply satisfying
I say "yes," even when a request is forcing me to sacrifice my boundaries	I will allow myself to say "no" to opportunities or requests that don't feel healthy for me
I'm very self-critical	I will practice owning my strengths and gifts
I regularly think "I'm not good enough" when I experience setbacks. Then, I berate myself for having negative thoughts	When I notice negative self-talk, I will respond with care, rather than criticism. I will take a moment to remember a time when I did something well. This is evidence that I can overcome other challenges
I'm making choices based on someone else's values of perfectionism and predictability	I will be more aware about living according to my own values, including simplicity, creativity, spontaneity, play and courage

Starting with your commitments is important for two reasons: You have an immediate way to orient toward self-loving choices and it roots your wedding day in a powerful purpose. Let's talk a little more about why each of these matters.

Orienting Toward Self-Loving Choices

Your commitments are a navigation tool. Whenever you feel uncertain about a decision, ask yourself: What would be most in line with my commitments?

Let's say you've just finished a challenging day of work and your friend calls to invite you out for pizza and beer. While that sounds fun, and you'd hate to let your friend down, what you think you need is a hot shower, a healthy meal, and an early bedtime. You feel your chest tighten as you try to decide what to do.

Then, you remember your commitment to take better care of yourself. Rather than push through your exhaustion, and end up even more tired the next day, you send a quick reply: *I love this idea, but I've got plans (with myself!) tonight. What if we go out Friday night instead?* Whew! By heeding your commitments, you're avoiding that all-too-common habit of overextending yourself.

Of course, you will not honor your commitments in every instance, and that's just fine. Aiming for perfection will not support your self-love and self-care, anyway. If ever you feel like you've thrown your commitments out the window, take a step back. Rather than beat yourself up, notice what happened and get curious about what you can learn from it. Keep in mind that self-love is a game without a final destination. Instead, with each month and year, you gather wisdom that makes you a better player and allows you to act in accordance with your commitments.

Commitments Root Your Wedding Day in a Powerful Purpose

After you identify your commitments, share them with trusted confidantes. Find a time and place where you can relax and be comfortable, then tell your friends or family about why each commitment is important to you and the difference following them could make in your life. Leave plenty of time for your loved ones to ask questions. Often, those questions deepen your understanding of what matters most.

Then, invite these witnesses to remind you of what you shared if you ever doubt your decision about self-marriage. This can help you avoid the trap of thinking your choice is about ego or getting attention. No. It is about something far bigger: a commitment to becoming the best version of yourself so you can also be the best version of yourself in relation to others.

Finally, keep your commitments where you can see them and review them regularly. They can be focal points in the vows you write and reading them occasionally will make sure they stay top of mind. To give you an idea of how powerful this can be not only in general, but on your big day, I'll share a personal story.

There are many beautiful commitments

Below are some of the commitments people made to themselves during their self-marriage:

- On the day of her self-marriage, Sarah Proffitt committed that she would never give up on herself again. No matter what happened, she wouldn't stop pursuing her dreams or goals. From then on, Sarah says she was better able to follow through on promises she made to herself. She credits this vow with helping her business grow and improving her health.

- During Teresa Trout's (37, Alameda, California, anniversary: 10/25/2014) self-marriage, her officiant asked a very poignant question: "Do you commit to choosing life in the darkest moments of fear, shame, guilt, disbelief, anger and rage? Do you commit to following through with this lifetime and not wavering in your commitment to yourself?" The words hit home. Just two years earlier, Teresa had voluntarily hospitalized herself due to deep depression and suicidal ideation. In her next chapter, Teresa was committed to rebuilding herself with next-level mental health support.

- Zoe Brooker committed to always checking in with herself about decisions. She wanted to live by this rule: "If I'm not a 'fuck yes,' then I'm a 'hell no.'" If things weren't clear, she committed to giving herself the space and time to process and tune in to her needs and wants. Finally, she committed to creating opportunities for her full self-expression and cultivating the courage to make the most of them.

- At a ceremony in her home garden, Robbie Fincham's commitments to herself included:

"I will stop and listen carefully to my intuition when it's trying to guide me,"

"I vow not to let lack of confidence get in the way of trying new things",

"I will try to remember that growth only happens when I step outside my comfort zone," and

"I promise not to beat myself up when I do not live up to the promises I make today."

- While looking at her reflection in a mirror, Hazel-Grace Yates (40, Nevada City, California, anniversary: 8/2013) committed to owning her beauty, power, strength, wisdom, truth and brilliance; to choose the lifestyle that would support her in blossoming into the most magnificent being she could be; and to bring loving compassion to her self-saboteurs.

- Bianca Eleanor (31, Essex, England, anniversary: 1/21/19) shared how she would be a better partner to herself in her vows. She said: "I promise to hold space for you, no matter what you are going through, and to witness you without judgment. I promise to allow you to process without trying to rush you. I promise to appreciate all your achievements more and demand less from you. I give you permission to do the things that ignite your soul and to turn within and rest when you are tired. I will be the one who makes you happiest and someone you can depend on. [That way,] you never need to look elsewhere to know how loved you truly are."

❖

The morning of my self-marriage, when my friend Michael walked through the front door, I immediately sensed something was wrong. His normally carefree gait seemed stiffer, and he was avoiding eye contact with me. Since Michael had been off running wedding errands all morning, I took a deep breath, expecting bad news.

"We have a slight problem with the cake," he said.

These are words no bride wants to hear, and, knowing Michael, "slight problem" had all the makings of an understatement. As a whitewater kayaker and the founder of a sizable startup company, he has a higher tolerance for unexpected setbacks than most. For all I knew, the cake was now a mutilated mess in the driveway, and he was developing a clever plan to secure another one.

I looked at him questioningly.

"Don't worry," he said. "I'll make it even better than before."

"Can I see the cake?" I asked hesitantly.

"I think it's better you wait."

My stomach dropped. Now I *knew* something awful had happened. At that moment I had a choice: I could let my worry take over, as it so often had in the past, or I could stick to the commitments I'd made: to accept when there was something I could not control and choose to see whatever unfolded as perfect. I took a few deep breaths, allowing my anxiousness to run its course. Then, I responded.

"OK," I said earnestly. "I trust you."

A few hours later, when I walked into the kitchen of my wedding venue, I was floored by the cake I saw. It was flawless! Not only was it exactly what I'd asked for (a two-tiered creation surrounded by spun sugar and with a miniature pumpkin on top), but it had a gorgeous flourish of autumn leaves running down one side.

"This looks amazing!" I exclaimed as I gave Michael a huge hug. "*Now* can you tell me what happened earlier?"

While transporting the cake home, Michael explained, the pumpkin had fallen off, crushing one side of the Pinterest-perfect dessert. To fix it, he had smoothed out the frosting and covered the pumpkin's war path with foliage from the garden.

Had I gotten upset, I realized, it would have been a waste of my energy. I would have spent half the day worrying about something that ultimately worked out just fine! By deciding to stick to my commitment of declaring everything to be perfect as is, I'd had a better experience and practiced a way of responding to challenges that I hoped to continue in the future. What an amazing gift to myself!

Sticking to your commitments is a valuable choice that will serve you during your self-marriage and beyond. When you use this approach, decision-making will become faster and easier. You'll have a guiding light to lead you through the fog of indecision. Like any new skill, proficiency will come through regular practice. Follow the exercises below to start to build your aptitude.

Self-Love Practices:

By yourself or with a friend, come up with commitments that feel nourishing and inspiring. To do so:

- Use the questions below to identify a few behavioral patterns, habits, or ideas that block your optimal experience of life. Then, write out commitments that would help you develop different tendencies.

  1. When are you unable to laugh at yourself?

  2. When does your self-care go out the window?

  3. When is it difficult to show yourself kindness and compassion?

  4. When do you sacrifice a little (or a lot) too much?

  5. When do you people-please at the expense of your own needs?

  6. What negative self-talk do you experience?

  7. How do you self-sabotage?

- Next, let's add to those commitments by looking at positive habits you can reinforce:

  1. What are you doing when you're at your best?

  2. What positive attitudes or ways of thinking support your resilience?

  3. What commitments would support that version of yourself more often?

- Finally, we look to others for inspiration:

  1. What have you seen other people do for themselves that you would love to emulate? For example, if you feel stiff and sluggish – as many of us do at one time or another – you could choose to take inspiration from a friend who committed to exquisite self-care. This might lead to eating more healthy meals, stretching regularly, exercising a few times a week, or getting a massage each quarter.

  2. What are your favorite songs about love? How can those lyrics inspire your own commitments?

- With your list of commitments in front of you, consider how your life will evolve if you actively practice living in this new way.

- Share your commitments and why they're important to you with at least one person.

- Begin to consider how you might incorporate your commitments into your vows. You'll have the opportunity to do a rough first draft of your vows in the next chapter.

Be gentle with yourself, learn to love yourself, to forgive yourself, for only as we have the right attitude toward ourselves can we have the right attitude toward others.
— *Wilfred Peterson*

Lulu Jemimah laughs with friends minutes before her ceremony.
Photo credit: Michael O'Hagan.

STEP 3:

DRAFT YOUR VOWS

C hicago (February 2011) – I sat staring at a blank page on my computer, the cursor blinking. It was four o'clock in the afternoon, and my editor was expecting a story about the Adler Planetarium's new exhibit in one hour.

I was still bundled up in the thick coat and beanie I'd worn while out reporting. It was a freezing day in Chicago, and I needed all the warmth I could get. As the minutes ticked by, the discomfort of the lingering chill began to pale in comparison to my mounting anxiety. This was *not* a moment for writer's block.

Can I do this? I thought, imagining the humiliation of missing my first deadline for Medill Reports, the media outlet for Northwestern University's Medill School of Journalism.

"We've got all the stories, except one…" I could hear the newsroom manager saying. "Where's Meg's piece?"

I felt nauseous picturing myself sitting there, the sole failure in our group of extremely competent graduate students. For all of us, the newsroom experience was a rite of passage: the first true test of whether we could make it as professional journalists. Writing compelling articles despite sweat-inducing time limitations was part of the job.

I envisioned the ensuing drama if this story went unwritten. I could see my advisor inviting me in for a "chat" about my future in the program, and my peers avoiding eye contact with me when professors assigned future group projects.

How the hell do I get this done? I wondered.

And then, seemingly out of nowhere, the answer arrived: *Just start writing.*

I felt a wave of relief as I began to jot down everything I could remember from my interviews and firsthand experience in the planetarium. Then, I grabbed my notebook and underlined my favorite quotes from conversations with the planetarium staff, visitors, and the real-life astronaut I'd had the honor to meet.

Half an hour later, I had a hideous first draft. More importantly, however, I also had a renewed sense of confidence. I furiously edited the piece, moving sections around, tightening my lede, and double-checking that I captured all the essential information. Five minutes before the 5 p.m. deadline, I emailed the finished story to my editor.

"Great work," she said, smiling when I approached her to check in. "Ready to do it again tomorrow?"

❖

Since my tenure in the Medill newsroom, I've gone on to write stories for many big-name publications, including *The Huffington Post, USA Today, Yahoo!,* and *Hidden Compass*, as well as to support professional and amateur writers in publishing their own stories. Based on these experiences, I know that composing anything – let alone your wedding vows – can be stressful, no matter your level of expertise.But don't worry. We start this process early so that you have ample time to put your thoughts together and refine your writing. Plus, in this chapter, I'll give you tips and tricks to make drafting your vows as easy as possible. You may even enjoy this assignment, since it will include reflecting on some of your favorite memories, your self-love journey, and how your commitments will shape your life moving forward. Stick with it, and you will not only have a heartfelt speech you're proud to share, but also a message to lean on whenever things get tough.

The goal with your first draft is just to write *something.* We want to keep the bar *super low* so that you don't put too much pressure on yourself. Thus, as you move through the following exercise, remember my morning in the newsroom. My first draft was the Quasimoto of news stories, but it gave me something to work with. Celebrate anything and everything you jot down as a fantastic starting point and know that you will refine the document over time (if perfectionism often blocks your self-love, this can be a particularly poignant practice).

Does writing your vows sound like a painstaking project?
Remember: You don't have to do it yourself. In this situation, self-love might mean delegating the task or going with the easiest option!

- Melissa Denton (46, Weymouth, England, anniversary: 6/1/2018), allowed her officiant to write her vows. She simply repeated after her while at the altar! If there is someone who knows you well and is gifted with words, they could be the perfect person to enlist for this job.

- Logan Griffin (35, Santa Barbara, California, 5/25/2005) wrote nothing ahead of time. Instead, when it was time to say his vows, he shared spontaneously. "I can't remember exactly what I said," Logan told me. "But it is the inner knowing in my heart that remains and matters most." Nevertheless, he could recall two key phrases that were important to him: "I love myself unconditionally" and "I'm whole and complete within myself." Even though he made up his vows on the spot, he said it was very meaningful to say them and be witnessed by his two friends.

- Gabrielle St. Evensen (55, East Coast USA, anniversary: 8/2000) loves to hold self-marriages for others. In fact, she's already married more than 1,000 people to themselves at various festivals around the United States. As part of the ritual, she offers each person a menu of vows, shown at the end of this chapter. Feel free to pull inspiration directly from this list!

Watch the interviews with Melissa, Logan, and Gabrielle here:

Answer the following questions

Journal about one or more of the prompts below. If writing isn't your thing, you can record yourself responding to the questions out loud as you take a walk or think through the answers with a friend.

- What are the most important lessons you've learned about yourself through your self-courtship or otherwise?

- What do you love most about yourself? (This could be an aspect of your personality, your favorite part of your body, or anything else)
- How will you better celebrate your accomplishments and strengths moving forward?
- Describe a moment in which you felt deep appreciation for who you are.
- Share one or two instances when you questioned yourself and how you overcame those doubts (or how you are working to do so).
- What is inspiring you to marry yourself?
- Why are your new commitments important to you?
- What do you believe will become possible in your life if you fully embrace these commitments?

Just. Start. Writing.

Now that you've gotten the creative juices flowing, it's time to distill them into the first draft of your vows. To make this as easy as possible, I'm giving you a simple framework (but don't feel pressured to use this if you feel otherwise inspired). It includes three parts:

- storytelling,
- takeaways,
- and promises.

I suggest your initial draft be done in stream-of-consciousness style. Then, walk away and celebrate the critical step you just took. You can edit everything later. The most important part here is to just start writing.

1. **Storytelling**

Kicking off with a story is a great way to start any speech (including your vows). It gets your audience engaged, and – since you're talking about your firsthand experience – it's easy to remember. The prompts above invited you to come up with a few stories you can use. Choose one to get started.

Example: I remember walking into the dressing room at Macy's and looking in the mirror. I immediately began to judge myself. "You've gained so much weight in the last six months. You'll need to drop a few pounds if you want anyone to find you attractive." I was on the verge of tears when I suddenly realized what I was doing: I was being my own worst enemy, rather than my best friend. I took a deep breath, walked up to the mirror and looked myself straight in the eyes. "How you talk to yourself matters," I said. "Let's try this again." I exited the dressing room and entered once more, this time with my head held high. As I strutted into that tiny stall with its bad lighting, I tried out a new inner dialogue. "Hey, gorgeous!" I said with a wink. "Let's find some clothes that compliment that lovely body of yours."

2. Takeaways:

Tell the audience about why that story matters to you, what you learned, and why you've chosen it to be a part of your vows.

Example: That moment was the first time I countered my negative self-talk, and it's made all the difference. As time has gone on, I've tried to nourish myself with the words and beliefs that support me, rather than ones that tear me down. This makes me feel so much better and allows me to pursue goals with greater confidence.

3. Promises:

What are you promising yourself now? This can include things you're leaving behind, as well as what you are aspiring to. This part should reflect your new commitments.

Example: Today I'm here to commit to standing up for myself with the same vigor that I do for others. While that moment in the dressing room was a first step, I'm ready to be a relentless proponent of my inherent worth, beauty, and abilities.

Marinate

After you've created your first draft, allow what you wrote to "marinate." Over time, return to your vows and update them as you feel inspired. You might get a great idea while you're out on a hike, finishing this book, or having dinner with friends. Allow space for that to happen! Remember, too, that your final draft may look *nothing* like the first one. That's just fine. This process is valuable because you will continue to explore what self-love means to you.

The Finishing Touches

In the final days before your self-marriage, put the finishing touches on your vows. Don't be afraid to ask for support from a friend if you'd like some brainstorming or editing help.Consider, too, how you want to present your vows. Do you want to say them directly to the audience? Would you like to say them to yourself in a mirror? If you are an artist or artistically inclined, you might consider turning your vows into a song or dance. The best option is the one that lights you up.

Meditation: An Access Point To Your Brilliance

For two of our interviewees, Jevranne Martel and Linda Doktar – meditation played a key role in writing and refining their vows. I asked these ladies to include more about their process, so you can try out this approach, too. If you decide to give it a shot, begin with something simple, such as just a few minutes of the practice. If the experience is fruitful, you can expand the time you spend on it.

For Jevranne:

To find inspiration for her vows, Jevranne expanded on her daily meditation ritual. In the week leading up to the wedding, she would go and sit next to a body of water. At first, it was a lake near her home. Then, it was the beach where she got married.

Jevranne faced the sun and, slowly raising her arms toward the sky, concentrated on all the love, positive energy and healing in the world. Next, lowering her arms and exhaling, she would push out any negativity, pain, or stress within her. "I did [this cycle] three to seven times, depending on how much I need it," she explained.

Jevranne then sat in stillness, thinking about who she was at her best, her soul, and her spirit guides.

"I'm about to write the vows," she would say. "If there's anything you'd like to jump in and add, I openly welcome that."

For Linda:

The week leading up to her wedding, Linda sat in meditation with herself each day and asked: "If I was operating from my highest truth and highest Self, how would I live? What promises would I make myself?" Based on the answers she heard, she continued to refine her vows.

When I asked Linda what else she wanted readers to know, she said:

"There is no 'right way' to meditate. It looks and feels different to all of us, and even to ourselves each time we practice. Meditation is about discovering your own unique style of being present with yourself and the now."

You can watch the interviews with Jevranne and Linda here:

~❖~

Despite knowing how stressful tight deadlines can be, I managed to wait until 8 a.m. on my wedding day to start drafting my vows. While I'd thought through the questions I shared above, I hadn't yet put pen to paper. Knowing my guests would arrive in a few hours was the motivation I needed to get cracking.

Sitting at the kitchen table with a big cup of genmaicha green tea and a bright yellow notebook, I felt the old fear of writer's block creeping in.

Pen to paper, Meg! I encouraged myself. *You know how to do this.* I flashed back to my desk in the newsroom where my interview notes had been strewn across my workspace. I knew all the pieces were in my head. All I had to do was start.

I smiled as I recalled one of my favorite memories: I was 10 years old and driving up into the Sierra Nevada Mountains with my dad. When he stopped the car, I wandered into a forest nearby and pretended I was on an expedition in a remote, foreign land. I felt beautiful, powerful and the excitement of being on an adventure. I wrote about that experience, and then moved on to the take-aways and promises:

"You knew in that moment you wanted to be a photojournalist and live in the mountains," I wrote. "Your intentions are powerful. You went on to become a photojournalist and to spend time with many mountains. You've since listened to your intuition and followed it to great success, despite what others thought or said. My wish for us is to continue our journey of self-love and self-actualization, to go beyond people pleasing and create a life perfectly aligned with our values. Let's stay wild."

To my surprise, the first draft was done in twenty minutes.

Was that too easy? I wondered. *Shouldn't writing my vows have been a longer process?*

Then, I smiled: making things complicated was not what my self-marriage was all about. In fact, it was one of the things I was committed to giving up. The vows were sweet. They were thoughtful. They were blissfully good enough.

I allowed myself another hour to edit. Then, I declared the vows finished. Reading them later that day, I brought myself (and several of my guests) to tears. It was not because my words were perfect, but because they came from the heart and truly meant something to me. My authenticity would make my expression impactful for me, and perhaps for others, too.

Through this experience, I discovered how saying your vows to an audience takes self-love from a solo endeavor to a community effort. My witnesses can now remind me of my promises, and they know about the moments in the past that made me who I am today.

This will be true for you, too. In opening up to those you trust, you will cultivate a group of advocates who support you when you feel intimidated about building the future you want. In this way, your vows are an access point to next-level community and personal empowerment.

Text box: A Menu of Vows

As promised, here are some of vows from Gabrielle St. Evensen's list. Before marrying someone to themselves, she offers them the chance to choose from these options or to create their own.

I promise to…

- Love myself like I love those whom I most treasure
- Know my genius and do things to remind myself of it
- Obey my small voice that knows the truth
- Do the right thing so I can live with myself in peace
- Forgive myself
- Expect the best from myself in spite of any old wounds from others who doubted me
- Understand my own signals for when I need help and get the help I need
- Know that I must occasionally revisit my values, priorities, work and relationships, and take measured steps to fix imbalances
- Accept that I am totally responsible for my own happiness.
- Bring sweetness into my life even when that seems far-fetched.

Self-Love Practices:

- Begin drafting your vows using the structure I shared above. Set a timer for five minutes for each section, and don't put your pen down until the timer goes off! The goal here is to just get your thoughts out. If you're struggling with this exercise, talk through each of the questions with a friend for five minutes. Make sure to record that conversation!
- Add material to your vows as you feel inspired, and reach out to people you trust if you need any brainstorming or editing support

- Set aside a block of time (no more than an hour or two) before your wedding to put the finishing touches on your vows and practice reading them out loud a few times. Remember: It's not about saying the right thing. It's about sharing what matters to you with people you love.

- Decide how you want to present your vows. Do you want to say them to an audience or into a mirror to yourself? Would you like to dance them or sing them? It's entirely up to you!

Love yourself unconditionally, just as you love those closest to you despite their faults.
— *Les Brown*

Robbie Fincham triumphantly walks down the aisle after marrying herself in front of an audience that included her daughters, friends, and neighbors.
Photo credit: Yen Seo

STEP 4:

DECIDE ON YOUR ATTITUDE

Chicago (May, 2012) – I refreshed my email for the tenth time, waiting for the message that would determine the next steps in my career. The day before, I'd had a stellar interview with a magazine company in Los Angeles. Given how well it had gone, I had a good feeling I would be their next hire.

"We'll be in touch by noon tomorrow," they'd told me. It was now 12:03 pm, and my impatience was turning into downright annoyance.

Of course, that's when the message popped into my inbox. I clicked on it quickly, ready to celebrate. Rather than details about our next steps, however, I saw the words I'd come to know well: *Thank you for your application, but we're going with someone else.*

I was sick of reading this line. Since finishing graduate school, I had been rejected by dozens of potential employers. And while the "no" always stung, the worst part was my growing sense of disillusionment. Each time I was passed up, I felt less hopeful that I could secure any job – let alone one I actually liked. Furthermore, I began to second-guess my worth as a journalist.

Of course, I'd been turned down for jobs in the past, but this much rejection was new for me. I was discovering that my job search was requiring more grit than I'd mustered previously, and my ability to endure was flagging. Thus, I slogged through the job application experience, eventually finding an exciting position in New York City. Even though I was relieved, the job came with a big red flag: It would require me to live in Manhattan on a $30,000 annual salary.

When I imagined myself living in one of the most expensive metropolises in the world on such a tight budget, I felt scared. I pictured myself eating rice and beans for most meals and moving into a tiny apartment with five other people. Thus, when I set foot in Manhattan a few weeks later, I was terrified. It was a painful end to a painful application process.

~❖~

When I think about this younger version of myself, I am overcome with compassion. She had no idea how to best prepare for the rejection that is often part of pursuing meaningful projects, whether it's a new job or self-marriage. She also did not have the tools to support a positive attitude when the going got tough. She was simply doing the best she could.

I also know that, if that younger version of Meg had received the bounty of criticism I received after my self-marriage, she would have reacted very differently than modern-day Meg. She would have felt embarrassed, second-guessed herself, or dealt with a spiral of shame that left her out of sorts for weeks. Instead, thanks to a technique I'll share with you here, I was able to quickly rebound after the negativity that came my way.

Because self-marriage is still relatively uncommon, you may *at least* get some raised eyebrows if you choose to talk about it. Rather than feeling disempowered, let's prepare you to flip this criticism on its head. You can have an attitude about negativity that fuels your self-love, rather than undermines it. Just imagine what will be possible if you master this skill, applying it to your ceremony and the other meaningful projects you undertake. You'll have some serious, next-level grit to keep you going!

It Can All Be Positive, Too

As we move through this chapter, keep in mind that criticism and negativity won't necessarily be part of your experience, especially if you don't speak about your self-marriage on national television!

Many of the people I interviewed received nothing but positive feedback. This was the case for Melissa Denton who celebrated alongside 130 wedding guests.

In the months leading up to the event, she said "You're welcome to be a part of my self-marriage, just choose whatever role you like!"

People volunteered to do various meaningful tasks. For instance, one friend stepped up to be celebrant and another insisted on giving Melissa away and singing a beautiful jazz song. This song was the soundtrack as friends and family threw confetti over Melissa after her ceremony.

"It was a collective effort," Melissa said. "In the months leading up to it, everyone was getting really excited about it! Who doesn't love a big party?"

Melissa said the entire day of her self-marriage was "perfect," from the ceremony to the vegan feast at the reception. Her guests were all supportive and had a great time.

Your attitude decides whether you suffer through your commitments or are fueled by them. Of course, maintaining the upbeat mood is easier said than done! We all know what it's like to feel down, want to take control, or get shaken by other people's views. Sometimes we may even overcompensate by trying to *make* everything positive, instead of cultivating our ability to *be* positive regardless of what's going on in the world around us.

When it comes to your self-marriage, your ability to choose your attitude in the face of others' opinions will be critical. For instance, you may have an outspoken sister who just hates carrot cake, but you've always loved it. How can you make sure that you enjoy your choice to the fullest, rather than get stuck in feelings about disappointing her? Learning to prioritize your preferences (and *feel good* about honoring them) will make sure you maximize your satisfaction that day. The following exercise will help you do that.

Gamechanger: Process Simulation

A 1998 paper from the University of California-Los Angeles, titled "Harnessing the Imagination: Mental Stimulation, Self-Regulation and Coping," shares how a method called *process simulation* can increase your ability to reach your goal. I've applied this approach to many different things, and using it was critical (or essential) when I faced the worst of the Instagram hate mail about my self-marriage. If it could get me through those moments, it can also help you when the going gets tough. Let's talk about how to apply process simulation so that criticism doesn't sting as much or linger as long.

Process simulation is shockingly simple. All it entails is a short exercise during which you imagine yourself taking the steps to achieve your aim. In our case: responding to challenges (whether it's your sister's opinions or a wedding cake disaster) with resilience.

In the original UCLA study, students who wanted a high score on an exam spent 15 minutes each day envisioning themselves diligently *preparing* for the test. After five to seven days, these students significantly improved their test scores as compared to the control group. Through process simulation, the researchers noted, subjects had strengthened their ability to better manage their emotional states, as well as to plan and solve problems.

Imagine what this could do in the carrot cake scenario. During process simulation, you could see your sister criticizing something in *the exact way you know she does*. Then, imagine yourself responding with the attitude of your choice. Perhaps, in this case, it's compassion and a steadfast commitment to your boundaries.

"I know you're not a fan of this flavor," you might imagine yourself saying. "I wanted to give you a heads-up before the event so you can bring a different dessert if you'd like one!"

As you imagine the play-by-play, your ability to respond in your desired way will improve. Any stress you have about addressing your sister's complaints will begin to decrease and you'll likely develop some additional ideas of how you'd like to handle the situation.

Through process simulation, you can thus increase the likelihood of gracefully handling challenges that arise.

Of course, there's a learning curve anytime you practice a new skill. Don't be worried if your visualizations feel challenging at first. Many studies have shown that visualization improves performance, so stick with it! Over time, this approach will strengthen your ability to choose your attitude and act accordingly, even in the face of your gnarliest critics.

Challenging conditioned beliefs

When Linda Doktar (37, Gold Coast, Australia, anniversary: 2/14/2017) livestreamed her self-marriage to share the message of self-love, she attracted more attention than she anticipated. Linda received invitations to speak from various media outlets. After doing so, however, she discovered her message about self-marriage was polarizing. She received messages of appreciation, as well as some full of hate and judgment.

Why does Linda believe people had negative reactions? Outdated belief systems.

"There is a collective belief that marriage should be between two people," she said. "But here's the thing: We shouldn't be just two halves coming together. If we can [find] wholeness within ourselves, we can show up in wholeness to a sacred union with someone else."

Anytime we publicly challenge the status quo, even if it's with a beautiful message, we will make some people uncomfortable. Luckily, keeping everyone else comfortable is not our job.

❖

I'd like to harken back to the beginning of this book. As you might remember, I mentioned that a little alarm bell went off in my nervous system when *This Morning*'s producers told me they had a psychologist available.

"You may get a lot of attention," they told me. "Let us know if you need anything."

Decoded, this meant one thing: There would be haters.

Knowing how vicious online trolls can be, I began to practice process simulation. I imagined receiving emails or messages that poked at my core fears, including that I was ugly, fat, or would die alone (Yup. It got dark) I saw myself objectively looking at these comments and, instead of feeling upset, celebrating on the phone with my friend Peter who had walked me down the aisle.

"I have haters!" I imagined myself exclaiming. "Doesn't that mean I've 'made it?'"

By the time my interview rolled around, I felt confident that I would receive some nasty messages, and that this would be OK.

I was not resigned to slogging through tough times. I had a way to prepare myself, and I'd diligently done my job to get ready.

I felt extra grateful for my efforts a few days after my segment aired. That's when one truly immaculate hate letter appeared in my Instagram inbox. What made it special, you ask? This person had taken the time to go back multiple *years* in my social media feed, and he had insulted many different parts of my life. He shared his opinions about my physical appearance, my ex-boyfriends, all the things I didn't deserve, and much more. His comments were bountiful and, all things considered, pretty darn creative. In terms of slander, this was A+ work.

For the briefest moment, I felt like I'd been punched in the gut. This was actually worse than anything I'd imagined. I took a deep breath and shook my body to clear the negative energy. I took a walk around the block. I drank a big glass of ice-cold water. Then, a glimmer of excitement entered my consciousness. Someone *had* done a lot of work to write that note. My talk about self-love had *really* gotten their attention.

I picked up the phone and dialed Peter, just as I'd practiced in my mind again and again. "Guess what!" I exclaimed. "I got my first hate mail!"

"...and you're *happy* about that?" he questioned.

"I am!" I explained. "This means my story is reaching people. For every person like that, there are dozens of others out there who *needed* to hear about my self-marriage and *loved* the segment."

You, too, have the power to turn uncomfortable situations into scenarios that

light you up. Through process simulation, you can learn to choose an attitude that supports your self-love and makes you the best possible steward for your self-expression. You can therefore be prepared if an insensitive relative shares an unsolicited opinion, a stranger rolls their eyes, or for any other challenging moment.

This ability to choose your attitude will also support the post-wedding bliss you deserve. It will help you build courage to embrace your authentic desires and trust you can handle any feedback. You are strong...and with practice, you can be even stronger.

Self-Love Practices:

1. Quickly answer the following questions. What attitude would you like to bring to

    a. ...your wedding planning process?

    b. ...your wedding day?

    c. ...people who give you unsolicited advice?

    d. ...people who give you unsolicited opinions?

    e. ...any haters?

2. Take note of any concerns you have about your self-marriage. Is there anything you're worried might happen before, during, or after?

3. Begin to practice process simulation for at least 5 minutes each day. See yourself choosing the attitude that would most serve you in a given scenario. Watch yourself move through challenges with power and grace.

4. Journal about the following question: If you developed your ability to choose your attitude in the face of challenges, how would your life evolve?

How you love yourself is how you teach others to love you.
— Rupi Kaur

Britt Lynn LaBouff poses in her borrowed wedding dress at the Dragonfly Ranch in Hawaii.
Photo credit: Barbara Moore

STEP 5:

CHOOSE YOUR PEOPLE CAREFULLY

N ew York City (September, 2013) – A man made his way toward me in the dimly lit dance hall, artfully stepping between couples who had already begun moving to the DJ's latest blues song. It didn't take me long to recognize this person with his distinctive, confidence stride: it was my good friend John.

I hopped up from my seat, improvising a series of rhythmic triple steps that complimented Ruth Brown's melody. John matched my moves, and we were soon within earshot of one another.

"Would you like to dance?" he asked me, smiling broadly as he extended his hand.

"Obviously!" I said.

Not only was John one of the kindest people I knew, but he was also one of the best blues leads in the world. Dancing with him was nothing short of dreamy.

John wrapped his arm around my waist, and I felt the warmth of his body as he pulled me into a close embrace. Trusting his guidance, I relaxed into my role as follower, allowing him to invite me into turns and tempo changes. As I went, I accented these moves with flourishes of my own. I closed my eyes and enjoyed feeling alone with just John and the music. Three minutes later, as the song faded into silence, I was in an elated daze.

"That was beautiful!" I exclaimed.

"It was!" John responded.

And with that, I knew it was time to broach the subject I'd been thinking about.

"Can I talk with you about something?" I asked.

"Absolutely," he said, as we took a seat off the dance floor.

"I want to be teaching dance more often, and I'm looking for someone to partner with," I said. "I really enjoy spending time with you, and I see you as someone who is dedicated, compassionate, and just plain fun. Do you have any interest in working together?"

He did, and over the course of the next year, John and I created and executed innovative programs filled with dancers from across the East Coast.

Throughout this experience, I would often pause and share my appreciation of John.

"I love doing this with you!" I would say after we'd taught an engaging class or enjoyed a joyful brainstorming session. "I feel so lucky."

But then again… it wasn't luck. I'd carefully chosen John as a partner, singling him out from many other talented leaders. In John, I'd identified a thoughtful collaborator, someone who respected me for my drive and vision, and a dance mentor who helped me elevate my skills while never making me feel inferior for having less experience. Making such a careful decision was an act of self-love, since I knew John would be an encouraging and positive presence.

❖

This experience drove home an important lesson that I carried with me into my self-marriage, and that I hope you'll carry with you into your own life: People matter. A lot.

Choose the right ones, and any experience will become richer. Choose your people poorly and you might spend more time justifying why you're marrying yourself than enjoying the wedding. Self-marriage, after all, is not *yet* a common event. Because of this, it may bring up confusion or concern for those who don't understand the concept.

When I shared the story of my self-marriage with my mom, for instance, she worried that others would think I was self-centered for doing such a thing. Had I told her my plans before the event, her fear might have rubbed off on me. There was enough to manage without that additional ball to juggle!

Instead, I invited *only* those who I knew, beyond a shadow of a doubt, would be unequivocally supportive (which is also the way I've chosen my closest friends). These ride-or-die attendees were my rocks when I started to feel nervous about something – and I'll share more about this at the end of the chapter.

For now, this is all you need to remember: You're allowed to be picky with your guest list and prioritize friends and family members who bring levity, compassion, and encouragement to those around them. Focus on people who are curious when they don't understand something, rather than judgmental, and choose guests who you sense will be excited about the idea of your self-marriage. It's better to have a small group of wildly supportive friends than a large group of people who are only half on board.

Bigger is not necessarily better

Sasha Cagen was living in Buenos Aires, away from most of her friends and family, when she decided to marry herself. Part of what made Sasha's wedding day so special was the help of one person she knew from the tango scene: Alexandra, or Ale. Ale had married herself previously and understood the meaning behind the ceremony.

"She was a coach for me," Sasha said. "She kept me accountable and helped me pick out my outfit and decide where to do it. She was also over at my place the night before, reminding me to take a bath with candles because this would be my 'last night as a single woman!'"

As you think about your guest list, remember that quality over quantity is a good approach for most people! Self-marriage is a vulnerable experience, and you need to surround yourself with allies who will treat it with the reverence it deserves. Anyone who is a "maybe" should be a "no." Guard your event with care so that, on your wedding day, you feel comfortable surrendering into the experience and speaking your mind. The safer you feel, the more present you will be. This will make sure you can revel in every powerful moment.

Pay extra close attention to those you invite to be in your wedding party. These people will be your first line of defense against second-guessing and doubt. They will remind you of your commitments and how powerful your attention can be.

Furthermore, asking for their support can be a great step toward improving your self-care.

Delegation is also an important expression of self-love that often gets neglected.

While delegating may feel uncomfortable, it can have a reverberating, positive impact on the way you go about your life. Use your wedding prep as a dojo for learning how to identify the people who will best support you and build your muscle around asking for help.

❖

"Can you come over early?" my friend Sara asked me. "I want to interview you so we have your words and intentions woven throughout the ceremony."

Sara was the first person I told when I decided to marry myself. Over the years, I'd come to know her as a creator of whimsical events, a thoughtful facilitator, and a proponent of authentic self-expression. I knew, therefore, that she would be delighted to hear about my idea and would likely be up for officiating the event.

Indeed, she'd happily agreed to do so, and was ready to put the finishing touches on her script.

Sara interviewed me as I applied my eyeshadow at the venue – a beautiful adobe house in Boulder, Colorado.

What do you love most about yourself?

What does this wedding day mean to you?

How do you want this ceremony to influence the rest of your life?

Sara was taking her job seriously, and the respect and reverence she brought to my self-marriage was contagious. As I took time responding to each of her inquiries, my appreciation for Sara grew. Her caring presence allowed me to think more deeply about the importance of the day and to thoroughly savor the hours before the event.

Roles your friends or family members can play:

- **Wedding brainstormer:** Feel daunted by planning? Have someone help you brainstorm all the details (we'll talk more about details in the next section).

- **Wedding coordinator:** You don't need to manage the event. If you have a Type A friend who geeks out on organization, they will love this role.

- **Cheerleader:** This is someone who will root for you before, during, and after your big day. The perfect candidate for this role is the person you call whenever you need a boost. They see you as the best version of yourself, remind you of how capable you are, and have kind words to offer when things feel challenging.

- **Officiant:** This is the master of ceremonies. They welcome guests and share the context of why everyone has gathered and what inspired your special day.

- **Ringbearer:** Someone must guard your ring until you put it on your own finger!

- **Relaxation angel:** This person reminds you to breathe and stay grounded throughout the wedding planning process.

- **Wedding Day Care Bear:** The person assigned to make sure you eat lunch and breathe deeply as you're getting ready and running between hair and makeup appointments.

- **Context holder:** Someone assigned to remind you of your commitments as you go through the wedding-planning process.

- **Person who walks you down the aisle:** Enough said!

- **Musician and/or DJ:** Choose someone who understands your taste in music.

- **Flower arranger:** This could be a professional florist, someone who can grab a lovely bouquet from a nearby grocery store, or a friend who loves to gather and arrange wildflowers.

- **Honeymoon planner:** If you're not excited about organizing your own honeymoon, give this role to a friend who loves planning or a professional travel agent. Make sure to tell them where you would love to go, your budget, how long you want to be there, and what you would like to do.

- **Cake master:** The person who will order and pick up your cake.

You can make up any other roles as you feel inspired.

Now, how do you request support? Here is a template you can use in an email or conversation:

Hey, [insert person's name here]. I have something to ask you, and it makes me feel a little nervous. I'm putting on a self-wedding because I want to commit to [share a couple of your commitments here]. This feels important to me, since [share why it's important]. I would love to ask for your support, if you're open to it? As I was imagining this experience, I saw you as the ideal person to [share the role you'd like them to have] because [share why they're your top pick!]. Would you be up for talking more about this?

Self-Love Practices:

These assignments are all about practicing the self-loving skill of asking for support. In these practices, not only will you make requests of others, but you'll also notice *how it feels* to make requests. Getting to know your default relationship with support is the first step in choosing the relationship to support what would best serve you.

- Create a list of invitees who you know will be delighted to support you. Remember, anyone who isn't an absolute "yes!" should be a "no."

- Write out your ideal team of wedding helpers.

- Reach out to each person on your list, tell them what you're up to and request their support.

- Journal about your experience asking for support.

  a. What was it like for you to ask for help? Why do you think that was your experience?

  b. What was it like receiving people's responses? Why might that have been your experience?

  c. How would you like your relationship to support to change in the future, if at all?

How can you include people you don't invite in your ceremony?

- While Sophia Kayla Treyger only invited her friends to her self-marriage, she carried a picture of her parents while she walked down the aisle. This way, their important part in her life was acknowledged.

- When Alex Christopher Strand married himself the second time (yup, you read that correctly!) he had only one witness: his officiant who was present via Zoom. Because many of his friends and family were in his home country of Iceland (and not his current location in Sweden), it was difficult for them to attend. To make sure he could share the experience with those he loved afterward, he recorded the ceremony.

- At her wedding reception, Laetitia Casano had a table full of important mementos, including a statue she'd carved of her grandmother and a picture of her with her mother. She wanted her lineage to be represented because not only did she love and appreciate her family, but she also knew that some of her negative self-love patterns were generational. Laetitia said she wanted to bless the new path of self-love for her family.

- Laetitia Ngueyen: Laetitia showed pictures of her wedding and gave a gift from her wedding location in Santorini to her supporters who couldn't come.

Remember to watch the interviews:

Be so completely yourself that everyone else feels safe to be themselves, too.
— Unknown

Alex Christopher Strand shows off his wedding band after his ceremony.

STEP 6:

HEED YOUR INTUITION TO IDENTIFY "HELL YES" DETAILS

Washington, DC (January, 2015) – Out of the corner of my eye, I saw someone opening the case of black-light body paint I'd left for my guests to find. When I'd set the paint on a side table earlier, I wondered how long it would take my friends to discover it. The answer: less than twenty minutes.

I tried to stay focused on the person in front of me, maintaining polite conversation, but I felt increasingly distracted by the magnitude of the moment: My party was about to take a turn for the epic.

Within a few minutes, people were decorating one another with neon yellow, pink, and blue designs, their laughter attracting more aspiring artists.

"Hey, birthday girl!" one of my friends called out to me. "Come here!"

As I skipped over to where the action was happening, I could barely contain my delight. This was all going according to plan, and I couldn't believe I'd hemmed and hawed about this magnificent purchase a few days earlier.

When I first saw the body paints in a store, I knew I wanted them. My intuition told me they would provide an extra dose of fun for everyone at my Saturday night shindig. Before I checked out, however, I'd had a moment of pause. My intellect was intruding on my gut instinct.

Is this excessive? I wondered. *Will people enjoy this or just think it's weird?*

I stood there for a good five minutes, second guessing myself. I even picked up the paints and then put them back on the shelf on a few times. That is, until the perfect question floated into my consciousness:

When has your intuition ever been wrong?

While I could remember times when analytical decisions didn't pan out (the pros and cons list only worked so well) or emotional decisions fell flat (I didn't often make sound choices when I was sad or angry), gut decisions seemed to work every time. Thus, while there were plenty of reasons *why not* to make the purchase, I decided to go for it.

Now, fifty people – many of whom had never met – were crammed into my home. Covered in bright colors, we danced to Prince and Michael Jackson songs until the wee hours of the morning. The paint united us.

While I did spend the next week cleaning up paint left in the oddest of places, it was worth it. The party was recorded in our collective history as one of the best. My gut had, once again, led me to the kind of "hell yes" detail that makes for fantastic memories. Next time, I promised myself, I'd act quicker on my gut instincts. That was a self-love skill I wanted to hone.

❖

We've all had those moments when something *just feels right*. Even if other people don't understand or agree with your choice, you trust it down to the marrow of your bones. In that instant, it's locked in. And – if you can brush off any second-guessing or doubt that may try to obscure this clarity – these sorts of decisions become a shortcut to your most satisfying, values-aligned existence. Heed these messages and you'll not just enjoy a fantastic self-marriage but shift from "meh" to "hell yes" in many other parts of your life.

While you may not perfect intuitive decision making before your wedding day, the planning process is a prime opportunity to practice this new way of moving through the world. As you look at various options for colors, venues, party favors and other parts of your wedding day, notice when there is something that *just seems right*. You might recognize it through a rush of excitement or a deep sense of knowing. It could also be that you instantly can visualize *that specific detail* as part of your ceremony. It's clear as day! Stay open to the various ways your intuition will speak to you, as it can differ from person to person. If you're paying attention, you'll soon discover how yours shows up (and I'll walk you through an exercise on this in just a bit).

If you're like most people, you will also quickly discover how fast the voice of fear or other people's opinions can drown out your intuition. In fact, you might have just a flash of it before you're second guessing yourself.

I have a name for these distractions. I call them "shoulds." "Shoulds" are a normal, predictable block to the massive self-expression that intuition makes possible.

Here are a few examples of "shoulds" that could emerge when you're planning your big day:

- Even though funk is my favorite kind of music, I shouldn't have a funk band because some people might not like it.

- Even though I'd love my wedding officiant to share a personal story about our friendship during the ceremony, I shouldn't ask her to do that since it might make her uncomfortable.

- Even though I love lots of color, I shouldn't decorate my yard with pinwheels because that might be too quirky.

- Even though I appreciate the finer things in life, I shouldn't include fancy gift bags because some people would think it's excessive.

- Even though I don't like to dance, I should have a wedding dance because that's what I've seen other people do.

- Even though my family hasn't been supportive of my self-marriage, I should invite them because that's the "right" thing to do.

As you can imagine, dozens more variations of what you "should" do exist. To help you turn down the volume on the "shoulds" and design a wedding full of "hell yes" details, let's talk more about how you can learn to heed your intuition. That way, you'll be able to recognize when others' opinions or your fears are running the show, rather than your true desires.

First, Give Your Intuition a Chance to Kick In

Expose yourself to different ideas, whether through wedding magazines, Pinterest, a wedding planner, or talking to other people. Your job in this phase is to notice your reaction to each suggestion. Note when something seems to speak to you on a deeper level. Compare this to situations when something just seems like a "good idea" (versus a genuine desire) or a detail your guests would like (versus what you truly want).

If you're susceptible to others' thoughts and opinions, you can start this process by yourself. That way, you have the privacy to explore your reactions without being influenced by anyone else.

Throughout this first part of the process, don't put any pressure on yourself to make final decisions. There is value in simply *observing* what comes up for you. Awareness is the first step to change. In this case, it's the first step to developing a closer relationship to your intuition.

Second, Clarify How Your Intuition Shows Up

As you pay attention, patterns will begin to emerge. Perhaps you get goosebumps every time you *really* like an idea. Or maybe you feel more relaxed and find yourself nodding when a detail seems like just the right fit for your big day.

In essence, you will start to understand how your intuition speaks to you. As I've worked with clients on building their intuition over the years, I've identified many ways this sixth sense manifests. These include, but are not limited to:

- A palpable gut reaction
- Deep, grounded inspiration
- A body sensation (warmth in the chest, relaxation of the shoulders, etc.)
- An inner sense of "just knowing"
- A hunch
- An urge to do something, even if you don't know why
- Feeling comfortable, even when a decision doesn't seem rational
- Inexplicable peace and certainty

- A feeling that something is missing or may happen

Typically, our intuition is the first reaction we have, and it whispers, rather than shouts. It's a wise, steady voice that remains present even if fears, emotions, or "why nots" pile on top of it or speak to us in a louder, more urgent voice.

As you seek inspiration for your self-marriage, pay attention to your reactions to different ideas. When you're feeling pressured by someone, how does that feel? When you see something that lights you up before anyone else offers their opinion, what's that like? You may notice, for instance, that the latter feels invigorating. Perhaps your energy levels go up and you feel like you can breathe more deeply. Get to know how your intuition feels, as it is different for everyone.

Third, try out a game

If including your friends or family in the process helps you access your intuition, you can play a game of "yes, and..." Here's how that might go:

> *You:* I love sunny, beautiful days, so I definitely want to marry myself in the summer!
>
> *Person 1:* Yes, and... since you love sunshine, you can have a bouquet of sunflowers!
>
> *Person 2:* Yes, and... you can also have a sunflower in your hair!
>
> *Person 3:* Yes, and... everyone can throw gold glitter that matches those flowers as you walk down the aisle!
>
> *Person 4:* Yes, and...you can include gold glitter on the invitations!

The idea is to go as quickly as possible, to move out of your head and into the moment. What comes out of your mouth may surprise you! Creativity will build and you'll stumble upon some things that feel like a "hell yes!" Write down those details and then sit with them. If it continues to feel good, you're on the right track. If you realize an option is a "should," take it off your list!

Fourth, When in Doubt, Choose Joy

It's difficult to hear your intuition when you feel pressured. In those moments, go do something that makes you happy. By settling your nervous system, you'll be better prepared to identify what you want. And—who knows?—you might just find the perfect color for your wedding bouquet while out walking past spring flowers or hear the ideal song for your first dance while enjoying a glass of wine with friends.

Fifth, Blurt!

Oftentimes, blurting helps bypass the mental chatter that can happen when we're making decisions (this is also why the "yes, and..." game can be helpful). If you need a different place to start with identifying your "hell yes" details, try answering the following sentence stems out loud in stream-of-consciousness style.

Remember: These answers aren't final, and they don't even need to make sense. Consider them clues to what will make your heart sing on your wedding day.

What is your "hell yes" when you think of....

...wedding size?

...guests?

...budget?

...wedding date?

...flowers?

...ring?

...event location?

...invitations?

...how to arrive at your wedding? (think bicycle, horse and buggy, limo, etc)

...outfit?

...wedding meal?

...cake or other dessert?

...wedding activities? (think speeches, first dance, etc...)

...party favors?

...music?

...transportation to be used to depart from your wedding? (on foot, car, helicopter, etc)

...honeymoon?

...if so, honeymoon details?

After answering these sentence stems, take note of what you learned and especially any "hell yes" details that popped up.

Let's Talk About the Bling

A ring is a talisman — a worn reminder of your commitment to yourself. It's also a ton of fun to pick out! For many of the people I interviewed, choosing their ring was a highlight of their self-marriage experience:

- Instead of a physical ring, Sophia Kayla Treyger (42, Portland, married herself on November 21, 2020) chose to tattoo the star of David on her finger. The star of David was important not only because of her Jewish heritage but also because it symbolizes the union of the masculine and the feminine, a theme in her life.

- Kyisha Williams' ring was a family heirloom. "My grandmother had a beautiful practice of buying jewelry and saving it for her grandkids," they said. "She had given it to me, and I had put it away." When Kyisha came across it one day while organizing their room, they knew it would be their wedding ring. It's a gold ring with a small diamond.

- Zoe Brooker ordered a custom-made ring from Etsy: a silver band engraved with flowers and set with four pink sapphires. When I asked about the significance of the pink stones she laughed and said, "I really like pink sparkly things."

- Amy Kayla (27, Austin, married herself in May 2021) took her engagement ring from her first marriage to a local jeweler. He removed the diamond stone and replaced it with an ethically sourced Burmese peridot. "It was an homage to past, present and future," she said. "There was no need to buy something new and this was a great symbol of self-love. You don't need to start a fresh, new person. Every day we're improving."

- When Melissa Denton decided to marry herself, she hopped onto Amazon and purchased herself a blingy, $30 ring with a giant, fake diamond. Because it wasn't well made, it broke off Melissa's finger a couple years after her self-marriage. "I didn't replace it," Melissa said. "I felt I was in such a happy place with self-love and open to finding love with someone else." In other words, she left her ring behind, but kept her commitments. Not long after, Melissa met her now-partner Royce and says she is happier than ever.

- Rather than have one ring, Sasha Cagen has had several over the years. These have included a red ring made out of wood (gifted to her by a Colombian friend who also married herself) and a silver ring purchased at a street fair in Buenos Aires. She chose to have several rings because she knew she had a tendency to lose jewelry. Rather than worry about one, irreplaceable symbol, she chose to see buying new rings as a chance to recommit to her self-marriage vows.

❖

One morning, as I was perusing wedding websites for inspiration, a photo stopped me dead in my tracks: A bride and groom were kissing as their guests blew thousands of bubbles all around them.

That! I thought. *I need* that!

I felt my heart beat faster. I felt a surge of energy move through my body. I began to envision how wonderful this addition would be. My intuition was giving me a clear message.

I immediately ordered a few dozen bubble wands and, as I finalized the delivery details, enjoyed a deep sense of satisfaction. It was done. The bubbles would be mine.

Sitting at my desk, I had a flashback to the similar sensation of *knowing* I'd experienced when I'd seen the body paint years earlier. This time, I realized, there had been no hesitation. I knew that my flash of inspiration and feeling of certainty meant I was on the right track. Since identifying these sensations years earlier, I'd had the opportunity to listen for and heed them many times.

Planning your self-marriage is a self-love journey, so be gentle with yourself as you explore what you truly want. Try not to stress about all those details. Instead, listen for the moments of "hell yes" and then give yourself the opportunity to honor them. You can apply whatever you learn to the rest of your life, so don't rush. Take your time, tune in, and see what arises.

Self-Love Practices:
1. Try out any of this chapter's exercises that inspired you.
2. Keep a list of your "hell yes" details. Add to it as you feel inspired.

A Case Study in Intuitive Decision-Making
When Hazel-Grace Yates first heard about self-marriage, she *knew* it was meant for her.

"Up until that point in my life, I'd experienced toxic and unhealthy relationships," Hazel-Grace said. "So, I said 'fuck it! I'm going to be with myself for the rest of my life. I want to make a commitment to myself and have a beautiful ceremony.'"

She wanted to feel empowered within herself and she believed this inner work would allow her to be more ready for a healthy partnership with someone else.

Hazel-Grace didn't bother looking at others' self-marriages for inspiration.

"I thought, 'this is my ceremony and I get to create it exactly how I want,'" she said.

At a party, Hazel-Grace saw a woman wearing a dress she loved. As it turned out, that woman was a designer who upcycled clothes. Hazel-Grace immediately hired her to create her wedding dress.

When she thought about where to have her ceremony, Hazel-Grace identified the spot instantly: the temple at Burning Man. She had experienced many pivotal moments there before, so it felt meaningful for her to hold it that location.

And when would she do it? There was a particular morning during which many ceremonies took place at Burning Man. Hazel-Grace knew she wanted her self-marriage to be a part of those events.

The details about her self-marriage came to Hazel-Grace almost instantaneously, which is how she said she knew her intuition was working.

"[When I feel my intuition] there is no thought, second guessing or doubting," she explained to me. "It feels like my body is already moving in a direction."

So how did all these intuitive decisions work out for Hazel-Grace? In her own words:

"It was, by far, one of the most powerful, incredible and potent days of my entire life."

Watch the self-marriage interviews here:

The worst loneliness is to not be comfortable with yourself.
— Mark Twain

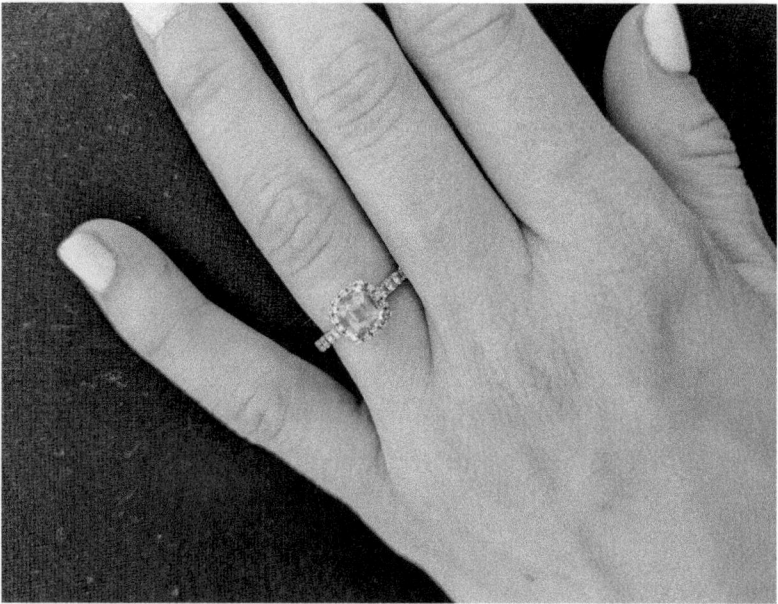

Amy Kaila shows off her wedding ring that features an ethically sourced Burmese peridot.

STEP 7:

Bring Intention to the Week Before Your Wedding

N ew York City (December 31, 2017) – It was 12 degrees Fahrenheit in Times Square, but that didn't stop me from taking off my coat for a photo op. Wearing a short, gold-sequined dress with sequined shoes to match, I looked the part of the quintessential New Year's Eve reveler.

I locked arms with my friends, and we all shivered as we smiled for the camera. The moment the picture was done, we threw our coats back on and rushed inside, just in time to watch the ball drop from our hotel room.

When the clock struck midnight, we were hopped up on free-flowing champagne and a sugar rush from too much Junior's Cheesecake. Confetti went flying, hugs were exchanged, and – just like that – 2018 had begun.

Shortly thereafter, I began to make my way around the room, trying quickly to say my goodbyes. I had a 6 a.m. international flight, and I wanted to get in a couple hours of sleep before I headed off.

"This is one hell of a final night you're having," said my friend Kyle as I gave her a squeeze. "I can't believe you're moving to the Dominican Republic tomorrow."

"Believe it!" I said grinning. "And come visit as soon as you can!"

The next morning, I groggily exited the hotel to find the streets of New York City silent, empty, and littered with streamers. I wondered at the contrast between this moment and the hullabaloo of the previous night as I waited for my Uber in the bitter cold.

When finally on my way to the airport, I sent some goodbye texts to people I hadn't had a chance to see. In the final weeks before my departure, time seemed to have sped up fivefold, and my best-laid plans to have an easeful departure had gone out the window. I still had boxes in the basement of my old house that would need to be dealt with later, and I wasn't sure that all my contacts knew I was about to become an expat. This concern was confirmed when I got a text back from a friend in Washington, DC. "Wait," she wrote. "You're *moving* moving?"

Yup... this clearly hadn't been the five-star transition I'd planned.

The need to improve my approach to planning became doubly clear the next week when, exhausted from back-to-back events, I contracted a terrible flu and spent my first week in the Dominican Republic too sick to get out of bed.

This wasn't how I'd hoped to kickstart my new life in the Caribbean. Moving forward, I promised myself I'd think more carefully about how to handle the days leading up to a big event. Lesson learned.

The week leading up to my self-marriage was thus carefully thought out (more on that soon). Likewise, the week before your wedding can be lovingly and carefully crafted so you feel your best on your big day. This way, you will be clear-headed and relaxed enough to soak in every moment. Plus, if you feel physically and mentally resourced, you'll be ready to bring your all to your vows, the dancing, and other parts of the experience. Your self-marriage will go by in a flash. You want to be ready to soak in every special moment!

With some intention, the leadup to your event can be a restorative time full of joyful reunions and exquisite self-care. That's right: the days before your self-marriage do not need to be stressful. Our goal is for you to *actually enjoy* each step of the process. Self-love is about celebrating the journey, not limping over the finish line on your wedding day, or anywhere else.

Since the final days before the wedding can pass quickly, here are some best practices for the week before:

Prioritize "you time": It is *not* excessive to have ample "you time" in the week leading up to your self-marriage. On the contrary, you will need to time to cultivate your peace of mind. This way, you're 100 percent ready for your big day. If you're not sure where to start, consider this question: When do you feel most relaxed? On pre-dawn walks? Nightly jogs? While sitting in meditation? Schedule these types of activities in so you have ample time to process and relax.

Hold a group check-in: One week before your self-marriage, find a time to sit down with your supporters and go through all the details. This way, items on the to-do list are less likely to fall through the cracks and you'll notice anything that's missing. Make this meeting fun! You can organize it yourself or ask a friend to arrange it. When in doubt, keep things simple: order in sushi, discuss everything over breakfast tacos at a local restaurant, or do whatever else feels nurturing and spacious.

Go on an appreciation rampage: One of the best ways to lower any pre-event stress is to focus on how much you can be grateful for. You are ready for next-level self-love! People have come to support you! You have a beautiful outfit to wear! You are in a lovely location! The sun has everything you appreciate.

Plan ahead for a more relaxing pre-wedding week

If you are having an event that includes lots of moving pieces, block out time in the two months before to finish the tasks below. For the most relaxing experience possible, finish these *at least* a week before your wedding:

- Clear your work to-do list so you can focus on wedding festivities
- Make a final wedding to-do list with the following items:
- Try on your wedding outfit. Make sure everything fits and is comfortable
- Pay your vendors in full
- Confirm drop-off times with vendors
- Finalize your vows
- Pack your must-have kit (makeup, hairbrush, small sewing kit, etc.)
- Confirm your hair appointment
- Send a "must have" shot list to your photographer
- Clean your ring...try it on? Admire it.
- Do a wedding venue walkthrough with: wedding planner...other people to whom you've delegated various tasks/jobs
- Assemble gift bags
- Plan your group check-in and send the details to your attendees

Check off final tasks: In the week before your wedding, here are the final tasks you may choose to take on or delegate:

- Steam your outfit, if necessary
- Get your manicure and pedicure a day or two before the event
- Check the weather forecast, especially if you're planning an outdoor event
- Decorate the wedding venue
- Practice your vows out loud and in front of a mirror
- Meet with your wedding support team to sort out any final details

Add to these lists as needed and continue to ask for an abundant amount of support.

❖

The sun was just rising over the Colorado plains as I walked along the gravel path. Each step I took made a satisfying *crunch*. The sound of my shoes on the gravel served as the soundtrack to an otherwise silent morning. Off to my right, I saw mule deer grazing in the foothills and a few tiny houses perched on top of the ridge, their windows still dark. This jaunt had been part of my daily "me time" since arriving in Boulder where my wedding would take place. It helped me stay grounded, even with my self-marriage just a week away.

Breathing deeply, I focused on the sensation of earth beneath my feet and the breeze on my face. Knowing that anxiety is created by dwelling on the future, I stayed focused on the present moment to find peace. This morning ritual was not about revisiting my massive to-do list. Nor did it involve wondering what might go wrong with the wedding logistics. This time was about centering myself so I was ready for my wedding day.

I recalled something I'd said to a client the previous week: Our attitude reflects how well we've cared for ourselves up until that point. Knowing this, I was taking my self-care especially seriously. I wanted to enjoy my big day as much as possible, and this meant making careful choices ahead of time. While I was tempted to cram in quality time with all the people who had traveled to attend my event, I also knew this was a recipe for exhaustion.

Rather than push myself to do *more,* I focused on how grateful I was for how I'd prepared for the week. This was a completely different experience than my departure to the Dominican Republic, as well as other less-than-graceful transitions I'd made in the past. I had set myself up to feel positive and healthy. Everything was organized, and I knew who would be taking care of each task. Furthermore, I'd only invited people who respected how important my alone time would be before my self-marriage. No one was pressuring me to attend gatherings or guilting me about not being more available. Everyone was off entertaining themselves and looking forward to the pinnacle event.

Gravel turned to cement as I made my way through a scenic neighborhood with gorgeous houses. Surrounded by wild grasses, large trees, and cacti, these homes were as lovely as the natural beauty that surrounded them. I walked slowly, admiring the large porches and big windows with views of the Rocky Mountains. I didn't have anywhere to be, and no plan for what else I would do that day. I might finalize a few more details, go for another walk or meet up for lunch with a friend... but all that could be decided later. For now, I just wanted to revel in the sense of spaciousness I'd created.

As your wedding approaches, set yourself up for a similar level of self-care. You do not need to feel beholden to anyone else's schedule. You have full permission to focus on your evolving desires. In fact, you are allowed – and encouraged – to do whatever you want. This time is precious, so treat it accordingly!

Self-Love Practices:

- *Consider what activities will allow you to feel centered in the week before your wedding.*
- *Schedule these activities, if desired.*

- *Think about what will make your group check-in and "me time" the most fun in the week leading up to your big day.*

How They Spent the Week Before Their Weddings

I asked our interviewees the following question: What sort of self-care did you do the week before the wedding to make sure you could be fully resourced, relaxed, and present for your big day? Their answers show there's no right or wrong way to prepare.

- The week before her wedding, Linda Doktar sat with her vows in meditation each day. This gave her the inspiration she needed to fine tune her words.

- Laetitia Nguyen arrived in Santorini five days before her ceremony. There, she enjoyed a hammam, body scrub, and facial to relax. This self-care made her feel beautiful inside and out. She also had time to check in with her wedding planners and explore the island with her guests.

- Leading up to her self-marriage, Britt Lynn LaBouff took part in a four-day movement and songwriting retreat at the Dragonfly Ranch on Kona, Hawaii. During this time, Britt Lynn unearthed several blocks to expressing herself authentically and committing to herself first. After the experience was over, Britt Lynn stayed an extra day to process what she'd learned. As she was discussing her takeaways with the retreat owner, Barbara Moore, Barbara asked Britt Lynn if she'd ever considered self-marriage. Barbara said she could help facilitate the experience and even offered up her own wedding dress! Although the pre-marriage self-care (and the self-marriage itself!) was unexpected, Britt Lynn said it was "divinely timed."

We do not have the right to feel helpless. We must help ourselves. After destiny has delivered what it delivers, we are responsible for our lives.
— Cheryl Strayed

Hazel-Grace Yates hugs one of the witnesses at her wedding at Burning Man.

STEP 8:

DON'T BE SURPRISED BY LAST-MINUTE CHALLENGES

Asheville, North Carolina (September 2020) —I listened intently as my client, Beth, recounted an intense conversation with her boss. Beth had just given two weeks' notice to her employer, and we were debriefing about her experience at a riverside café.

"I'd imagined many different ways the conversation could go," Beth said, sipping her coffee. "*That's* why I was so surprised by her reaction. It wasn't any of the scenarios I'd considered."

"What happened?" I asked.

"She said I was an asset and offered me a big raise."

"How did you respond?"

"I had to pause," Beth said. "It was really tempting. But then I remembered what you said: there's often one, final test before the breakthrough."

"So, you stuck to your guns?"

"I did," Beth responded, her voice steady. "I want to focus on the work I'm meant to do. It's time to start my business."

Beth's experience confirmed one of my theories about change: When you're on the precipice of a personal evolution, the universe will often dangle something *extra* enticing in front of you, just to make sure you're ready for the shift.

But are you really, really sure? That alluring opportunity or object says.

Other times, the universe presents a hurtle. For instance, the German chocolate cake that appears just after you commit to giving up sugar for one week.

Holding Her Ground

Laetitia Casano planned to have a beach wedding in Barcelona, but rain was forecast for the day of her ceremony. Her friends – who had the best of intentions – suggested she change the date.

"I said, 'Are you kidding me?!'" Laetitia exclaimed. "The date of my marriage is engraved on my wedding band, and I am picking up the flowers! Would you ask someone who is marrying someone else to change the date because it's inconvenient?"

Her friends later thanked her for modeling self-love in the form of boundaries.

"They said it was a good lesson in choosing yourself," Laetitia said.

In that moment, to overcome the last obstacle, you must trust you're on the right course and stay committed.

As Beth and I continued to chat, I realized this was also a reminder *I* needed. As my wedding day drew nearer, it was inevitable that last-minute challenges were right around the corner.

Rather than worry about what would go wrong, I decided to anticipate the imminent setback with curiosity. What would it be?! How quickly would I recognize it? How much care could I bring to addressing the challenge in a self-loving way? Whatever it was, I would do my best to lean into the opportunity.

❖

You may also encounter last-minute obstacles before your self-marriage! Remember that, as a hero draws closer to her treasure, she faces bigger and bigger monsters. Facing these foes – whether it's a two-headed dragon or an outspoken critic – becomes an opportunity to buckle up your rhinestone combat boots and gain valuable experience.

Furthermore, your wedding day is the last stand for many of your sub-optimal self-love habits, and these old ways of thinking and behaving may put up a fight. Don't let yourself be surprised! Instead, consider embracing one or more of my favorite pre-wedding mantras:

- Final setbacks are a sign I am on the right track.
- Solutions abound.
- If it's not what I originally hoped, it will be something better.
- I respond to obstacles with curiosity and grace.
- I surround myself with incredible people who are delighted to help me.

- I accept the abundant love and care that's offered to me.

Mantras are taught in Buddhism, Stoicism and Taoism, as well as in many personal

development programs. It's less common, however, that teachers highlight research that demonstrates their effectiveness.

A 2015 study published in the scientific journal *Brain and Behavior* suggests why mantras are so useful. When participants repeated a phrase, they had a marked decrease in brain activity. This meant the parts of the brain typically dedicated to planning and self-focused thinking were suddenly dialed down. In this way, subjects simply didn't have the mental space for obsessing. According to the researchers, this meant mantras had a "calming effect" on the mind.

If you've ever helped plan an event, you know that a dose of calm provides welcome relief. With all the to-do's, it's easy for stress levels to skyrocket. So why not prepare yourself for the inevitably intense moments by finding a sentence you like that will keep you grounded? Any unexpected challenges can be met with a soothing phrase that reinforces your self-loving paradigm, rather than second-guessing or a frantic attempt to solve an issue.

A Case of Cold Feet

The night before her self-marriage at the Fringe Festival in Brighton, England, Sophie Tanner was surprised to realize she felt nervous. Her ceremony would be a public affair at the world-renowned, heavily attended event. Given that the day kicked off with a choreographed dance procession, of which she was a part, she knew many eyes would be on her.

"It suddenly struck me that this may be more life-changing than I thought," she said during our interview. "[I realized] this is actually quite a big statement I'm making."

To calm herself down, she decided to cancel her evening plans with her bridesmaids. She had an early night instead and promised herself that, if she still felt as bad in the morning, she could always cancel the event.

She woke up the next day feeling clear that she wanted to move forward. She had dreamed of her self-marriage being a deeply impactful experience and she was ready. What a great reminder that self-care is critical to overcoming the one, final challenge between us and our goals.

❖

"There's no champagne," my friend and wedding photographer, Geof, said hesitantly as he looked in the fridge.

"Oh no!" I exclaimed. "I knew we forgot something."

It was an hour before my ceremony, and I felt the sudden urge to *fix this problem.* I, the bride, could handle it! I would just go pick up the champagne myself, looking gorgeous in my fancy dress and coiffed 'do. That made sense, right?

My building frenzy was suddenly interrupted by the realization that *this* was the final obstacle. I started to laugh, eliciting a look of confusion from Geof.

"What… just happened?" he asked.

"I was about to hop in the car and go to the store," I said. "But that doesn't sound very self-loving. I think it would make more sense to have someone else do that."

Geof grinned. "I agree," he said. "Let's call David. He's on his way here, and I'm sure he can stop and pick up some bottles."

While I knew *I* could have gotten the job done, "handling things" was not my responsibility that day. It was part of my old, self-defeating habits of not letting others care for me and being on the go until I was over-tired.

Less than half an hour later, David showed up with an abundance of bubbly. Although I'd worried this request might feel like an imposition, it hadn't. David said he was thrilled to support me, and that the bottles were a wedding gift.

This lesson bears repeating: When you are about to take your life up a level, challenges will arise to test your resolve. While I had done an excellent job with my self-love up until this moment, the universe had one final test for me. In allowing myself to ask for and receive support, I'd passed with flying colors.

Self-Love Practices:

- Decide on a mantra you can use when the going gets tough and post it somewhere so you will see it every day. Feel free to use one of the mantras I listed above:

  - Final setbacks are a sign I am on the right track.

  - Solutions abound.

  - If it's not what I originally hoped for, it will be something better.

  - I respond to obstacles with curiosity and grace.

  - I surround myself with incredible people who are delighted to help me.

  - I accept the abundant love and care that's offered to me.

The Final to-do's

Below is a wedding-day checklist for you and your supporters.

For your supporters:

1. Double-check that all vendors dropped off items (cake, flowers, etc...)
2. Make sure food and beverages are ready to go (stocked, chilled, etc...)
3. Make sure all hired personnel have the event address, time, and contact info (caterer, bartender, photographer, DJ or musicians, etc...)
4. Feed the bride or groom breakfast
5. Feed the bride or groom lunch
6. Make sure all the support staff is ready, willing, and able to arrive on time

For you:

1. Review your vows
2. Allow yourself to be cared for by others
3. If you're having hair, makeup, and/or nails done, revel in the experience!
4. Practice gratitude
5. Stay hydrated
6. Cry when you want to
7. Laugh when you want to
8. Admire yourself in the mirror

I must undertake to love myself and to respect myself as though my very life depends upon self-love and self-respect.
— Maya Angelou

Laetitia Nguyen is ready for her solo wedding in Santorini, Greece, May 2017.
Photo Credit: Alexander Hadji

STEP 9:

HAVE A BLAST ON YOUR HONEYMOON

S an Diego (May 2021) – "I'm cancelling my honeymoon!" I called from the living room.

"What?" my good friend and wedding guest, Sarah Tilbor, said sleepily as she emerged from her bedroom. "Why?"

My stomach rumbled angrily.

"Remember those surf-and-turf tacos I was so excited about?" I asked. "They've come back to haunt me."

Sarah and I had planned our trip to Southern California with three goals in mind: to eat as many tacos as possible, spend quality time together, and partake in a fantastic honeymoon weekend to celebrate my self-marriage. While my special event would include plenty of alone time, I also loved the idea of sharing parts of the experience with one of my nearest and dearest.

Now, however, the long-anticipated weekend was off to an unfortunate start: the very same tacos I'd envisioned savoring had thrown a wrench in my plans.

Sarah came to sit with me on the couch.

"Maybe celebrate when you feel better?" she suggested sweetly. "I bet you can reschedule your solo activities and we can change our dinner reservation to another date."

I sighed. I didn't want to spend my honeymoon suffering, but the idea of postponing it was very disappointing. I'd saved up and been dreaming about this special weekend for months. Now, rather than journaling in cute cafés and wandering around the honeysuckle-scented streets of La Jolla, I would spend the day recovering.

If I'd just had a nice salad at home, this never would have happened. I thought. *I should have known better.*

Feeling let down, I was looking for someone to blame, and the easiest person to target was myself. Luckily, just as a wave of negative inner dialogue threatened to engulf me, I realized what was happening.

How many times had I beaten myself up over bad luck or an honest mistake? Too many. I wasn't willing to do it again now.

I stood up, shook out my body and took a deep breath. Standing tall, I imagined how I would respond if my future partner got sick on the first day of our honeymoon. Would I treat *him* with bitterness? Absolutely not! I'd get him soup and propose a fabulous movie marathon of whatever films he liked best. I needed to treat myself the same way.

"'I'm really sad," I told Sarah, allowing myself to feel the emotion at the root of my distress. "I was looking forward to everything. I guess it's time to take my vows to heart. I said, 'in sickness and in health,' and that means taking care of my body today."

"That's right," Sarah said. "And I'm here to support you, too."

Sarah then headed into the kitchen to make me some peppermint tea. While this wasn't the self-love experience I had been anticipating, it was the one I needed for now.

❖

This little incident had a fruitful ending. Instead of doing the things I'd planned, I lounged around, watched plenty of *Gilmore Girls*, and thought about why I felt so let down by the turn of events. In truth, I'd done a killer job planning my honeymoon and didn't want to wait!

I realized I had great advice about creating a self-love getaway to remember, so I began to journal. By the end of the day, I'd arrived at the conclusion that the best honeymoon is one that's tailored to your values, desires and needs. If you can take stock of these things, and plan accordingly, you will have an extremely satisfying experience.

So, what exactly are your values? Desires? Needs? Have you thought about that lately? Because these factors are critical to your personal fulfillment, they're worth considering. Let's dive into each area to explore how to make your honeymoon (and your life) all the sweeter.

Your Values

For a moment, I'll share how my values helped determine my honeymoon. I treasure beauty, connection, adventure, play, and self-care. These values led me to design a weekend that included:

- Thai massage
- Yoga
- Delicious, nourishing food
- Hiking
- Quality time with friends
- Journaling
- Dancing

Take a minute to jot down your own values. If you're not sure where to start, here's a brief list:

Sponta-neity	Trust	Play	Potency	Joy
Peace	Commu-nity	Connec-tion	Friend-ship	Compas-sion
Adventure	Beauty	Abun-dance	Flow	Nurturing
Dedica-tion	Openness	Wonder	Wisdom	Vitality
Originality	Resource-fulness	Generos-ity	Gratitude	Celebra-tion
Courage	Creativity	Ease	Hospital-ity	Learning
Self-Care	Delight	Power	Embodi-ment	Sensuality
Attune-ment	Pragma-tism	Charity	Collabora-tion	Fun

Use the list you created to inspire your planning. If you were to *only* consider these values – rather than what others think you should do – what would you plan? You can also make this a game: how many of your values can you include as you create your perfect getaway?

Your Desires

Our values are often at the root of our desires – the things we most wish for. Understanding your desires and owning them is a behavior that takes courage. Sometimes we hide our wants not only from others, but also ourselves. It's as if they were something to be ashamed of! Or like our inclinations are misplaced!

This is not the case. Your desires are core to your self-expression and self-actualization. You can see them as guides that lead you toward fulfillment. When you honor your desires, you are sending yourself an important message: you deserve to be happy.

Consider this when you plan your honeymoon. If you enjoy luxury spa days, add one to your agenda! It doesn't matter what others think. After all, most people wouldn't consider it over-the-top for a honeymooning *couple* to go to a beautiful resort, get a couples massage, and enjoy a fancy dinner. For many, the *point* of a honeymoon is to create space to honor a duo's desires. Allow this to be the case for you, too.

If you're unclear about whether a desire is authentic or something you feel you "should" do, ask yourself the following questions:

- Does this desire match my values?
- At the end of this experience, how satisfied will I feel on a scale of 1–10?
- Do I notice any tension in my body or negative emotions when I think about investing my precious time and energy into that activity?

Practice identifying your desires and do your best to enjoy indulging them. These skills are underdeveloped in our society, but they're worth building. Expanding your capacity for joy bolsters your ability to be your true self and support others.

As you go through your honeymoon (and life thereafter), keep in mind that desires are dynamic. Give yourself permission to change your mind. The goal of your honeymoon is to practice next-level self-love, not to stick to a certain itinerary.

You might notice, for instance, that you don't want to go to the movie you've already bought a ticket for. Rather than feel guilty for wasting money, celebrate the awareness that you don't want to go!

I don't desire it anymore! You can say jovially. *How wonderful that I see that!*

Then, think about what would *truly* light you up. Do *that* thing.

Remember: Your honeymoon is a special, dedicated time to practice over-the-top self-love. Use this experience to explore how much satisfaction you can allow yourself each day. Notice, too, if this incites any negative self-talk. This is normal. Because the human brain likes what it knows, it does all it can to keep you in familiar territory. Unfortunately for many of us, familiar territory is an underwhelming amount of self-love. It's time to fire up your jetpack and rocket out of that comfort zone, baby!

Have compassion for any concerns that arise and see if you can turn the "desire dial" up at least 5% each day. How can you honor your wishes just a *little* bit more?

Your Needs

Your needs are the fundamental component of your well-being and meeting them makes self-love sustainable. For instance, you may stay within a certain budget during your honeymoon to support your need for financial health. Similarly, while you may crave a second dessert, it may better fit your physical needs to take a post-dinner walk instead.

Your needs define the healthy boundaries of your desires, making sure self-love does not become overly hedonistic in a way that undermines your self-care later. Indeed, identifying and appreciating your needs will support your mental, emotional, and physical health during your honeymoon and beyond.

Make a list of your top needs for your honeymoon experience. How will you need to treat yourself so that you most enjoy every minute of that time? Some ideas include:

- Taking plenty of "me time" in the morning before meeting up with friends
- Prioritizing sleep
- Not rushing from one event or activity to the next

Take time to think about your values, desires, and needs before your honeymoon so you're best prepared to have your ideal experience. I credit this paradigm with helping me rock my own honeymoon... which finally took place after I recovered from food poisoning.

Choose your Own Adventure

As you tap into your values, desires and needs, you'll discover your ideal honeymoon scenario (which might even be forgoing one!). Here's what a few of our interviewees chose:

- Sophie Tanner saved up for two years to realize a lifelong dream of seeing gorillas in Uganda. She traveled alone, but met up with a friend for part of the trip.
- Bianca Eleanor kept her honeymoon simple: She carved out plenty of time for herself the week after her wedding. At home, she did things such as take crystal baths. This ritual involved filling her tub with hot water, essential oils, flowers, and – of course – a few crystals (morganite for universal love and rose quartz for self-love were two of her favorites). She turned off her phone and set up her music before she began to make sure this time with herself wasn't interrupted. If her mind drifted toward lists or chores, she would focus on giving thanks to her body or asking herself the same questions she would ask someone else on a date: How are you today? Shall we plan something fun next week?
- Linda Doktar didn't take a honeymoon. Immediately after the ceremony, she headed home for some alone time. She wanted to be present with herself for the rest of the day. Over the next few

hours, she reflected on her self-marriage and meditated on the path she was choosing.

❖

Sarah and I held up our glasses of Prosecco, ready to toast after the weeklong wait for my honeymoon to begin. Now that my stomach felt better, it was time to enjoy a good meal.

"Here's to *me!*" I said playfully.

"To *you!*" she said, smiling. "Those tacos couldn't keep you down!"

We sipped our bubbly and watched the passersby in San Diego's Little Italy peruse the local restaurants. It was a busy, sunny Saturday, and our dinner would be followed by a beach bonfire and an early bedtime.

"What part of self-love are *you* working on right now?" I asked Sarah.

"Trusting myself," she replied. After testing the waters in a few different cities, Sarah had just decided to settle in Denver.

"I've always wanted to live in Colorado!" she added. "It can be scary to choose and commit to a decision, but that's a gift I'm giving myself."

Since my self-marriage, I'd treasured the opportunity to have regular conversations about self-love with others. This seemed to be a topic that people were grateful to discuss – a welcome change of pace that left everyone feeling thoughtful and inspired.

My chat with Sarah was interrupted as our waiter set down plates of tempura squash blossoms, pistachio-pesto gnocchi, and pasta Bolognese in front of us. As we ate, we regularly paused to savor mouthfuls of the rich, savory dishes. Soaking in these special moments – the laughter, the flavors, and the rich orange hues of the California sunset – was an important piece of my self-love for the weekend.

"In a way, I'm glad I had to wait so long for this honeymoon," I said, as we both took our last few bites. "Seeing it as an upcoming event on my calendar continually reminded me to check in on my commitments from my vows. With a honeymoon, I think it's less about *exactly when* you do it, and more about the intention. This has been a great time for me to celebrate my commitments and reflect on how far I've come. Thank you so much for being here with me."

"Happy honeymoon!" Sarah exclaimed smiling. With that, we paid our check and headed off for our next adventure.

It deserves repeating: The best honeymoon is the one that is responsive to your deepest values, desires and needs – including those that arise unexpectedly. Considering each of these will allow you to create a post-wedding event that might be just as special as the wedding day itself. During this time, be so good to your body and soul that you come home glowing. Your honeymoon is a sacred opportunity to set a new standard for how you treat yourself (and – spoiler alert – it will also change the standard for how you expect to be treated by others!)

Self-Love Practices:

- Create your lists of values, desires, and needs.

- As you plan your honeymoon, refer to these lists.

- If you would like prompts to help you brainstorm about your ideal honeymoon, here are a few questions to explore:

  - What do I *really* want on my honeymoon?

  - ...and what do I really, really, *really* want?

  - And if I had all that, what would make my honeymoon experience be...

    - ...10% better?

    - ...50% better?

    - ...100% better?

  - How can I make honoring these desires *fun* for me?

Self-love doesn't mean that everyone will treat you the way you deserve to be treated. It means that you won't let them change the way you see yourself; nor will you stick around for them to destroy you.
— Tony A. Gaskins Jr.

Melissa Denton is showered with confetti after her self-marriage.
Photo credit: Sadie Osborne

REMEMBER THE OCCASION – POST-NUPTIAL RITUALS

A tlanta (July 2021) – I sighed deeply and rolled my shoulders back. I'd felt increasingly tense as I worked on editing the chapter you are reading now. I needed a break.

Throwing on a pair of tennis shoes and a jacket, I headed out to enjoy an early spring day. As I sauntered past rows of cherry trees, I admired how their bright, popcorn-ball blossoms looked against the backdrop of dark thunderstorm clouds. It was a familiar sight, and one that typically brought me a sense of peace.

On this particular day, however, it wasn't working. Rather than feel more centered, I could sense my stress levels rising.

What's going on? I asked myself.

And then it hit me: I was scared.

While I'd felt called to write this book, the act of publishing it meant putting myself "out there" in a vulnerable way. Anyone reading *Self-Marriage* would know far more intimate details about my wedding, beliefs, and desires than I'd made public previously.

While I knew I could handle additional hate mail, that didn't mean I *wanted* it. My concerns, I realized, must have been simmering in my subconscious all this time. Now, they were surfacing. I was on the final chapter of this book and the prospect of finishing it suddenly seemed much more daunting.

Is this crazy? I wondered, zipping up my jacket as a chilly breeze brushed my neck. *Other people have had way more impressive self-marriages than me. And what about all those people who thought I was just "an attention-seeking nut job?" They're going to have a field day with this.*

My inner dialogue grew increasingly pessimistic and critical… until I noticed I was absentmindedly fiddling with my wedding ring. As I ran my thumb over the smooth white-gold band and seven tiny diamonds, I focused on my commitments to myself:

- To trust my intuition and follow my gut despite what others might think

- To diligently continue my journey of self-love and self-actualization
- To move beyond people-pleasing and create a life aligned with my values
- To stay wild and have fun
- To choose to love myself even in the difficult moments
- To cultivate a richer, deeper, kinder relationship with myself
- To care for myself in every moment

Reciting my commitments was part of my morning ritual. While I knew it was good for my mindset in general, I didn't realize it would become a way to interrupt negative self-talk. Yet that's the purpose it was serving now! The work I'd been doing on self-love was obviously sinking in, and my rituals were helping the positive change stick.

❖

Rituals are powerful ways to influence your behavior, according to the 2013 *Scientific American* article, "Why Rituals Work." In this story, two behavioral scientists Francesca Gino and Michael I. Norton at the Harvard Business School define ritual as "the symbolic behaviors we perform before, during, and after [a] meaningful event."

According to Gino and Norton, studies show that ritual can increase confidence, motivate greater effort, and improve performance. In my case, the rituals I'd created after my self-marriage were helping solidify the promises I'd shared in my vows. The wedding *and* the reinforcing components were the combination that led to change.

My rituals included a few things:

1. Admiring a framed photo of myself from my wedding: I do this each morning just after I wake up. While I look at the photo of myself dancing through bubbles, I channel the emotions I felt on that day.

2. Saying my vows out loud to myself in the mirror once a week: I say these vows *with emotion.* This is important to ensure that the words I lovingly wrote to myself aren't forgotten and don't become a mere memory.

3. Touching my ring every evening: After admiring the white gold band that symbolizes my eternal relationship with myself, I say the name of each person my diamonds represent (everyone in my immediate family, plus a diamond for my future partner).

I also am planning to have an anniversary getaway each year, which will be my time to reflect and treat myself with all the care I deserve.

Ritualizing reminders of your self-marriage is an important step to making sure your new commitments stick. Your wedding day, after all, is not when everything gets fixed. Just as you wouldn't expect your future partner's imperfections to disappear when you tie the knot, you shouldn't expect your own to go away! A relationship with anyone – including yourself – blossoms over the years. With intentional work, you become a better and better fit.

❖

Obviously, I finished editing the book. After my challenging day, I turned my work into a weekday ritual. After rolling out of bed, I'd make a class of genmaicha green tea and dig into editing for a few hours. Then, I let myself have the rest of the day free to coach my clients, exercise, and practice other types of self-care.

By creating post-wedding rituals to remind yourself of your commitments, you increase the likelihood that your self-love goals will become your reality. The paradigms you want to embrace about your self-worth, boundaries, prioritizing yourself, and more can thus change from a good idea to a way of life.

Similarly, by introducing rituals around other goals, you are better prepared to realize other dreams. Whether it's writing one blog post a week for your business or starting a workout club to reach your fitness goals, you can leverage your rituals to create an aligned, inspiring and purpose-filled life.

Self-Love Practice:

- Decide on a ritual you would like to try out after your wedding day. You can change this ritual whenever you'd like to.

There Are Many Ways to Remember

Here's some inspiration for how you can keep your commitments top of mind, as well as further integrate the promises you made to yourself.

- Kyisha Williams proposed to themselves on November 3rd and got married on January 3rd. To remind themselves of their commitment, they decided to do something self-loving on the third of each month. This might be writing themselves a letter, choosing to have a light workday, or simply going on a nice walk by the water (which can be a rare treat for Kyisha as a mom!).

- Teresa Trout has a daily ritual with her ring. At night, she takes it off. In the morning, as she puts it on, she says "I love you." She also has an extended ritual that runs from her anniversary on October 25ths to January 1. During this time, Teresa creates a vision board, as well as takes stock of the challenges and wins from the last year. She considers what patterns she might be stuck in, what behaviors she wants to cultivate in her life and how else she wants to shift and change.

- After his simple and intimate ceremony on a beach accompanied by two close friends, Logan Griffin decided to remarry himself every day for an entire year. "I realized if I did it every day, then every day would be my anniversary and a reminder of this choice for the rest of my life," Logan said. Logan worked his self-marriage into his meditation each morning, during which he chose to love himself and to be deeply committed to himself no matter what happened.

- Gabrielle St. Evensen wears the red dress she donned at her self-marriage to other people's weddings as a secret way to wish them good luck.

- Britt Lynn LaBouff developed ongoing practices to further integrate her vows. One aspect is rituals timed around the cycles of the moon. During specific moon phases, she takes time to ask herself questions such as: What am I feeling challenged by? What am I ready to let go of? If I let go of those things, how would that impact my relationship with myself?

- Laetitia Casano regularly does mirror work – a methodology created by the self-love juggernaut and motivational author Louise Hay. She spends time looking at herself in the mirror and saying things like "I love you" and "you look beautiful." These messages reinforce her self-love and counter the negative messages she heard growing up, both from others and from herself.

- After her self-marriage, Linda Doktar hung her vows on her fridge. She kept them there until she felt like she was living by the promises she'd made to herself.

Other ideas include:

- Throwing a self-love party each year for your friends and family in which everyone shares something they love about themselves.

- Eating the top of your wedding cake a year after you marry yourself (make this conventional wedding tradition your own!).

- Writing yourself a love letter on your wedding day reflecting on the ways you've grown in the past 12 months.

- Each week, writing one of your commitments on your bathroom mirror with a dry erase marker or lipstick. This can become your tooth-brushing mantra.

- Printing your vows on a coffee mug. Before you drink your first cup, read through them.

- Revisiting sweet messages in your guest book each month.

> *If I'm not good to myself, how can*
> *I expect anyone else to be good to me?*
> — Maya Angelou

Teresa Trout shows off one of her cakes from her self-marriage.

THE END?

I learned a useful adage in my first life coach training program: With relationships, you're either building them, killing them or letting them die. In other words, coasting is a myth. If you want to nurture the best connection possible (with someone else or yourself), you must continue to cultivate love.

As I interviewed people for this book, I heard the same message repeatedly: *Self-love is a work in progress. The journey never ends.* The vow "for better or for worse" exists for a reason. There will be hard times in your self-marriage and life in general. If you consistently tend to your self-love, as well as remember to care for yourself when the going gets tough, you will be better prepared to weather self-doubts, fear, and other challenges with grace.

Self-marriage is one step in the self-love adventure. It offers an opportunity to pause and take stock of your self-love experience to date. Then, you consciously choose where you want to go. If you do not figure out how to integrate your new ways of thinking and behaving into your life, however, you my backslide. Lasting change comes from ongoing, caring attention. Don't miss out on the deeper transformation that is possible!

If you choose to move forward with self-marriage, let me know! Tag @self_marriage_book and @megantaylormorrison on Instagram so that I can celebrate you! The commitment to greater self-love is one that deserves to be highlighted and appreciated.

May we all remain cognizant of the power we have to shape our lives and remind one another of this fact when we forget.

Let's start a self-love revolution, shall we?

> *"Owning our story and loving ourselves through that process is the bravest thing that we'll ever do."*
> — Brené Brown

Sasha Cagen's self-marriage ceremony took places at the Japanese gardens in Buenos Aires, Argentina.

Appendix A: Self-Love Journaling Prompts

On my wedding day, my friends gave me a journal full of self-love journaling prompts that they wrote themselves. I've added in a few of my own, as well, and these are now my gift to you. I hope they will support you in continuing to explore self-love.

Something I'm learning to love about myself is...

A part of myself I want to grow is...

Something I'm ready to accept is...

Something I'm not ready to accept is...

The best thing about my day is...

I love myself by...

I up-level my self-love when I...

I know where my boundaries are when...

My favorite way of honoring my boundaries is...

I feel most alive when...

Today, what I appreciate about my body is...

I want to honor what I've learned from my past experiences by...

If I could have the answer to any question, what would I ask?

An adventure I want to go on is...

Something I haven't shared with someone close to me is...

My relationship to my power is...

One way I want to grow my power is...

My relationship to my beauty/attractiveness is...

I feel most beautiful/handsome when...

My dream house would have...

I feel at home when...

The part of myself that hasn't gotten enough attention lately is...

Time seems to stop when...

Something I'm ready to let go of is...

Something I'm not ready to let go of is...

Life loves me, and my evidence of that is...

My spiritual self is calling me to...

My sensual self is calling me to...

My playful self is calling me to...

My body craves...

My intellect is asking for...

My heart is yearning for...

The things I most under-appreciate about myself are...

My favorite food is..., and what that says about me is...

What my 10-year-old self would love about me is...

What my 18-year-old self would love about me is...

What my 25-year-old self would love about me is...

What my 80-year-old self would love about me is...

Appendix B: Bios for Those Interviewed

Many of the people I interviewed provided their bios:

Bianca Eleanor: Bianca is a stone medicine practitioner and educator, offering crystal transpersonal therapy and crystal acupuncture. She lives in Southend on Sea, England, with her husband and two young sons.

Britt Lynn LaBouff: Britt Lynn co-hosts the Sacred Sister Podcast and is an energetic cartographer and personal transformation coach. She guides those thirsting to map and transform their innerSelf.

Dr. Hazel-Grace Yates: Hazel-Grace is radical permissionist and pleasure warrior here to help eradicate global toxic sexual shame. She is endlessly passionate about humans celebrating their bodies, soul, and sex. She works as a somatic sex coach and educator.

Kyisha Williams: Kyisha is a Black, non-binary femme dreamer, filmmaker, actor, and health equity consultant. They fuse public health and digital media by creating socially relevant content that discusses health, as well as promotes healthy sexuality and consent culture. Kyisha is deeply committed to Black and Indigenous joy, health, and freedom. Read more at Kyishawilliams.com.

Laëtitia Nguyen: Laëtitia grew up in the French Alps, but later lived in seven countries around the world. After her solo wedding in Santorini, she became a full-time writer after being a finance manager for a decade. Visit her website: www.blogaboutl.com.

Laetitia Casano: Laetitia is a self-love intuitive guide. Read more about her and her work at https://msha.ke/femmedivine.

L. Gabrielle Penabaz (Gabrielle St. Evensen): Gabrielle is a multi-media performance artist and bilingual voiceover talent. Among her many projects she is a priestess in her ongoing one-on-one theater production, "Til Death Do You Part. Marry Yourself!" She has married over 1,000 people to themselves. Read more at EncouragingPriestess.com.

Linda Liv Doktar: Linda is an entrepreneur and success coach. Read more about her at https://lindadoktar.com/

Logan Griffin: Logan is an Intuitive Energy Healer, Yogi, Spiritual Guide and Life Coach. His work is dedicated to the healing and evolution of humanity through the personal healing, empowerment, and enlightenment of the individual. For more information visit: www.logangriffin.com

Lulu Jemimah: Lulu is a Writer and media consultant from Uganda. She completed her BA in media and film at Macquarie University in Australia and her Masters in creative writing at the University of Oxford in the UK.

Melissa Allen Denton: Melissa is a partner and director of medical supplies at Medisave. She lives in Weymouth, UK with her two amazing kids and partner.

Robbie Fincham: Robbie, an Australian civil celebrant, established *"Marrying Me"* in 2021. She offers bespoke self-marriage ceremonies to people wanting to commit to their own personal growth and happiness.

Sarah Proffitt: Sarah is a spiritual advisor and energy medicine facilitator. Read more about her: https://www.sarahproffitt.com/

Sasha Cagen: Sasha is the author of *Quirkyalone: A Manifesto for Uncompromising Romantics* (HarperCollins). This landmark book put a new twist on being a discerning single and got attention from many news outlets, including the *New York Times* and CNN. Sasha works as a life coach helping people who are drawn to the quirkyalone philosophy of not settling in life or love.

Sophia Kayla Treyger: Sophia is a radical pleasurist and intimacy coach. She serves spiritual women, couples, and her community by unprogramming bullshit beliefs, facilitating the release of trauma from the body, and teaching courageous communication.

Sophie Tanner: Sophie is a PR specialist and the author of *Reader I Married Me.* Follow her on Instagram @TheSologamist

Teresa Trout: Teresa is an expressive arts therapist who specializes in working with childhood trauma, inner child healing, relational challenges, sexual healing, and non-traditional relationships. She believes in the healing power of the creative arts to support individuals in rediscovering their authentic selves. Find her online: www.teresatrout.com

Zoe Brooker: Zoe is a licensed occupational therapist who enjoys taking her knowledge of meaningful activities, movement, and mindfulness into different areas of practice. In 2014, Zoe married herself, which had a profound effect on her life. Since then, she has offered courses and individualized support with a desire to help people own their power, self-worth and inner wisdom.

Watch all the interviews here:

About the Author:

Megan Taylor Morrison (Meg) is a science journalist turned Professional Certified Coach (PCC), best-selling author, and international retreat host. In her free time, you can find Meg soaking in icy rivers or competing internationally in lindy hop (the original form of swing dancing).

Meg trained in ontological, facilitative, and somatic coaching with institutions including Accomplishment Coaching, the Co-Active Training Institute, the Strozzi Institute, and Authentic Revolution. In addition, she completed an 18-month private mentorship with a leading executive coach in Silicon Valley. Meg is also Wim Hof Method-certified instructor.

Meg brings a unique combination of thoughtful structure and play to her work. She supports teams, leaders and entrepreneurs in reaching their goals while having as much fun as possible. Meg works one-on-one with a small number of private clients, runs annual business mastermind groups, and heads her virtual coworking community. You can read more about her at www.megantaylormorrison.com.